Brodie's Notes

C000195190

List continued overleaf

List continued from previous page

Harper Lee	**To Kill a Mockingbird**
Laurie Lee	**Cider with Rosie**
Christopher Marlowe	**Dr Faustus**
Arthur Miller	**The Crucible**
Arthur Miller	**Death of a Salesman**
John Milton	**Paradise Lost, Books I and II**
Robert C. O'Brien	**Z for Zachariah**
Sean O'Casey	**Juno and the Paycock**
George Orwell	**Animal Farm**
George Orwell	**1984**
J. B. Priestley	**An Inspector Calls**
William Shakespeare	**Antony and Cleopatra**
William Shakespeare	**As You Like It**
William Shakespeare	**Hamlet**
William Shakespeare	**Henry IV Part I**
William Shakespeare	**Henry IV Part II**
William Shakespeare	**Julius Caesar**
William Shakespeare	**King Lear**
William Shakespeare	**Macbeth**
William Shakespeare	**Measure for Measure**
William Shakespeare	**The Merchant of Venice**
William Shakespeare	**A Midsummer Night's Dream**
William Shakespeare	**Much Ado about Nothing**
William Shakespeare	**Othello**
William Shakespeare	**Richard II**
William Shakespeare	**Romeo and Juliet**
William Shakespeare	**The Tempest**
William Shakespeare	**Twelfth Night**
George Bernard Shaw	**Arms and the Man**
George Bernard Shaw	**Pygmalion**
Alan Sillitoe	**Selected Fiction**
John Steinbeck	**Of Mice and Men** and **The Pearl**
Jonathan Swift	**Gulliver's Travels**
J. M. Synge	**The Playboy of the Western World**
Dylan Thomas	**Under Milk Wood**
Alice Walker	**The Color Purple**
Virginia Woolf	**To the Lighthouse**
W. B. Yeats	**Selected Poetry**

ENGLISH COURSEWORK BOOKS

Terri Apter	**Women and Society**
Kevin Dowling	**Drama and Poetry**
Philip Gooden	**Conflict**
Margaret K. Gray	**Modern Drama**
Graham Handley	**Modern Poetry**
Graham Handley	**Prose**
R. J. Sims	**The Short Story**

General editor: Graham Handley MA PhD

Brodie's Notes on Edward Albee's

Who's Afraid of Virginia Woolf

Gavin Selerie BA MPhil
Tutor, Extra-Mural Department, University of London

Acknowledgements

Our thanks to Jonathan Cape and Edward Albee for permission to quote from *Who's Afraid of Virginia Woolf?*

First published 1988 by Pan Books Ltd

Reprinted 1992 by
THE MACMILLAN PRESS LTD
Houndmills, Basingstoke, Hampshire RG21 2XS
and London
Companies and representatives
throughout the world

ISBN: 0-333-58039-7
ISBN13: 9780-333-58039-4

Printed and bound in Great Britain by
CPI Antony Rowe, Chippenham and Eastbourne

Contents

Page references in these notes are to the Penguin edition of *Who's Afraid of Virginia Woolf?*

In the commentary/notes section the acts have been broken into shorter units, according to the natural alterations of pace (as where a character leaves the stage). This is to enable students to pinpoint phrases and speeches more directly.

Preface by the general editor

The intention throughout this study aid is to stimulate and
guide, to encourage your involvement in the book, and to
develop informed responses and a sure understanding of the
main details.

Brodie's Notes provide a clear outline of the play or novel's
plot, followed by act, scene, or chapter summaries and/or com-
mentaries. These are designed to emphasize the most important
literary and factual details. Poems, stories or non-fiction texts
combine brief summary with critical commentary on individual
aspects or common features of the genre being examined. Tex-
tual notes define what is difficult or obscure and emphasize
literary qualities. Revision questions are set at appropriate points
to test your ability to appreciate the prescribed book and to write
accurately and relevantly about it.

In addition, each of these Notes includes a critical appreciation of the author's art. This covers such major elements as
characterization, style, structure, setting and themes. Poems are
examined technically – rhyme, rhythm, for instance. In fact, any
important aspect of the prescribed work will be evaluated. The
aim is to send you back to the text you are studying.

Each study aid concludes with a series of general questions
which require a detailed knowledge of the book: some of these
questions may invite comparison with other books, some will be
suitable for coursework exercises, and some could be adapted to
work you are doing on another book or books. Each study aid
has been adapted to meet the needs of the current examination
requirements. They provide a basic, individual and imaginative
response to the work being studied, and it is hoped that they will
stimulate you to acquire disciplined reading habits and critical
fluency.

Graham Handley 1991

The author and his work

Edward Albee is the most significant playwright who has appeared in America since Tennessee Williams and Arthur Miller. Always searching for new modes of expression, he has at times alienated the critics and the commercial theatre audience. Nevertheless, he is a precise craftsman and his plays are consistently well made. Influenced by Strindberg, Ionesco and Genet – all in their way avant-garde – Albee retains a liking for the light stylistic touch of Noel Coward. *Who's Afraid of Virginia Woolf?*, his sixth published play but first Broadway production, excited great controversy and quickly became a modern classic. Profound in its analysis of human relations, and reaching back to the ritual origins of drama, it dazzles the spectator with a series of routines that are at once disturbing and entertaining.

Albee was born in 1928, the year before the Depression. Abandoned by his natural parents, he was adopted at the age of two weeks by a couple who were heirs to a famous vaudeville theatre chain. He was brought up in an atmosphere of wealth and luxury but became a problem child who would not settle at school. He was from the start surrounded by theatre people and he was taken to shows regularly. After years of conflict with his parents and an unfinished stint at university, Albee entered the bohemian world of Greenwich Village, New York City. Because of the terms of a family trust fund, he had to make his way doing odd jobs for another ten years. During this time he immersed himself in the radical artistic scene and began to write seriously. He developed a particular interest in the theatre of the absurd (that which deals with the senselessness of the world by non-rational means – as in the work of Ionesco and Beckett).

His first success was *The Zoo Story* (1959), a one-act play about an encounter in a park. Jerry, a social misfit, converses with Peter, a seemingly balanced and prosperous figure. Increasingly the meeting becomes an interrogation and a power struggle (literally at one point for space on a bench). Jerry, the aggressor or awakener, ends up impaling himself on a knife that he has induced the other to hold. Peter's middle-class security and conformity have been challenged in a grotesque but illuminating way. *The American Dream* (1961) also attacks complacency and materialism through a surreal vision of the normal. We see a family isolated in the living room of a stuffy apartment, waiting for the arrival of somebody who will carry out an (unspecified) household service. In a bizarre sequence of anecdotes, arguments and actions, the twisted background of relationships is laid bare. Mommy, whose adopted child disappointed her, is a caricature of the consumer-oriented matriarch. Daddy is an acquiescent, ineffectual figure, lost in the world of work. Only Grandma excites our sympathy. Language battles are played out in a way that foreshadows *Virginia Woolf* (1962) – hovering between fantasy and reality.

Later plays include: *Tiny Alice* (1965); *A Delicate Balance* (1966); *All Over* (1971); *Seascape* (1975); *The Lady from Dubuque* (1980); and *The Man Who Had Three Arms* (1982). Albee has also adapted novels for the stage, such as Carson McCullers' *The Ballad of the Sad Café* and Vladimir Nabokov's *Lolita*. His plays have been performed all over the world and there have been some notable productions in London. He won the Pulitzer prize for drama in 1967 and again in 1975. Both *Who's Afraid of Virginia Woolf?* and *A Delicate Balance* have been made into successful films, the former starring Richard Burton and Elizabeth Taylor. In the mid-1960s Albee used part of the profits from *Virginia Woolf* to fund experimental theatre in New York, thus fostering the careers of other playwrights.

Albee's work presents a sharp critique of the dominant social values in America (and perhaps of the Western world in general). He is adept at exposing the spiritual emptiness which can underlie institutional activity – particularly the family gathering. Hypocrisy, greed and pretence are deftly delineated. On the other hand, Albee does not display the moral or social commitment of, say, Arthur Miller. Rather, he creates a puzzle in which each position is relative. Like Harold Pinter, Albee emerged from a long acquaintance with theatre and, as an aspiring dramatist, found himself preoccupied by form – the devices and routines of role-playing. One imagines that the expressionist elements in *The American Dream* have their origin in the vaudeville shows that Albee saw as a boy.

Albee's plays involve extreme situations, ritual activity and ironic humour. Character and dialogue tend to be more significant than plot. At the creation stage, Albee tries to develop the identity of his characters before placing them in particular circumstances. His dialogue has a poetic or operatic feel (with aria-type monologues, duets and choruses). The learned is combined with, or set in opposition to, the trappings of a mass culture.

For example, in *Virginia Woolf*, the Carthage references and burial service excerpts recall the work of T. S. Eliot, while the Big Bad Wolf nursery rhyme (set to the tune of 'Here We Go Round the Mulberry Bush') draws on an early Walt Disney cartoon. Heavy ideas and social situations are explored with sharp wit (the comic co-existing with the tragic). The plays are usually economical in structure, having a small number of characters and requiring a basic (but expressive) stage machinery. *Virginia Woolf* and *A Delicate Balance*, despite their complexity, come close to observing the unities of action, time and place. Albee has denied the relevance of biographical data to any interpretation of his work, on the basis that an author 'writes from a whole complex of things.' Nevertheless, the details of his upbringing cast an interesting light on his preoccupation with such themes as the oppressive mother and the adopted son.

Who's Afraid of Virginia Woolf? is Albee's most successful fusion of naturalism (i.e. lifelike description) and stylization (artificial or symbolic description). The play is a triumph of theatricalism (zany dialogue and spectacle) which is, nevertheless, anchored in human habit. The language, as elsewhere in his work, mixes cliché with rhetoric, the colloquial with the formal, the staccato with the diffuse. The rhythms are controlled so as to produce an overall coherence. Albee has compared playwriting to the art of musical composition. He relies more on talk than action but physical movement, when it comes, is crucial and distinctive. Linguistic imagery is carefully linked to the stage set.

At various times Albee has been accused of unclarity, mystification and unnecessary morbidity or grotesqueness. His later work has not had the commercial appeal of *Virginia Woolf* or *A Delicate Balance*, perhaps because of its decreased emphasis on plot and characterization and its inflation of the language element. People have missed the sense of urgency which informed Albee's early and mid-period writing. However, Albee has always been one step ahead of his critics and his audience: few could have predicted the light, whimsical character of *Seascape*. In grappling with new topics and techniques, the playwright is bound to encounter opposition. The great artist charts the almost-unknowable. As Albee has said (with reference to *Who's Afraid of Virginia Woolf?*): 'I don't write reassuring plays . . . I'm not interested in the kind of problems that can be tied in a bundle at the end of the third-act curtain. You walk out of that sort of play, and all you can think about is where you parked your car'.

Background and setting

The action takes place in the living room of a couple who live on the campus of a small college in New England. This part of the United States, in the east, was the first to be colonized by Europeans, and it retains a certain old-world flavour in its landscape, architecture and attitudes. The town is called New Carthage, which has symbolic overtones (see below). The couple are called George and Martha, which suggests that, on one level, they are representative of the American dream of liberty, unity and equality (see the link with the Washingtons, explained below). George is an associate professor of History. Martha is the daughter of the founder and president of the college.

The titles of the three acts indicate that a ritual is to be played out against the initially cosy setting of the living room. In fact, *Virginia Woolf* is a series of stage games which echo the psychological and social games that we play in real life. As George and Martha interact with their guests, Nick and Honey, we pass from contests which are innocent amusement to those which threaten life itself. The stage time (three and a half hours) is more-or-less equivalent to the period portrayed (from two a.m. to the moments before dawn).

Critical commentaries, textual notes and revision questions

Act One: Fun and Games (pages 11-18)

Martha's first word ('*Jesus*') as she staggers through the door sets the tone for what is to follow: a series of verbal battles involving much raw language. She and her husband have been to a welcoming party for new faculty members, given by the college president. The couple have already had plenty to drink and it is late, but it emerges that Martha has invited two of the newcomers home. George is annoyed that she has issued the invitation and they quarrel. Martha has already criticized him for not participating fully in the night's entertainment. She has also launched into the first knowledge-contest in an argument about films. Such information battles are appropriate to the college setting. It is evident that Martha is the dominant partner, at least on the surface, and that George prefers to take a back seat. Nevertheless, he is a sharp and witty arguer; when roused he can be as cutting as his wife. As George sulks, Martha tries to divert him by repeating a gag she has used at the party – the singing of 'Who's Afraid of Virginia Woolf ...' to the tune of 'Here We Go Round the Mulberry Bush'. He is only mildly amused by the routine (which later comes to have symbolic significance).

cluck A stupid or naive person (i.e. sounding like a hen).
Bette Davis The famous American film star who specializes in roles that involve vitriolic wit – a posture which Martha characteristically adopts.
orgies Drinks parties for the staff (see page 23).
Georgie-Porgie, put-upon pie Comic variation on the traditional rhyme: 'Georgie Porgie pudding and pie,/Kissed the girls and made them cry;/When the boys came out to play,/Georgie Porgie ran away'.
Who's afraid of Virginia Woolf ... A parody of the nursery-rhyme 'Who's Afraid of the Big Bad Wolf' (see discussion of the play's title under 'Themes'). Virginia Woolf is the English novelist (1882–1941). On the last page of *Between the Acts*, published just after her death, Woolf describes a marriage as follows: 'Before they slept, they must fight; after they had fought, they would embrace. From that embrace another life might be born. But first they must fight, as the dog fox fights with the vixen, in the heart of darkness, in the fields of night.' A nursery-rhyme is recited at intervals earlier in the book.
simp Simpleton.
considering how old you are Martha, as we learn from the character

notes, is fifty-two, six years older than George.
firsty Imitation of child's pronunciation of 'thirsty'.
cipher A nonentity (from the character 0).

Act I (pages 18-25)

As the guests arrive George utters a key warning: that Martha
must not bring up the subject of 'the kid' in public. After some
delay, Nick and Honey are ushered in; they form a complete
contrast to the experienced, middle-aged couple. Nick is young
and athletic; Honey is a girlish, rather plain blonde. They try to
make polite small-talk but they are drawn into the arena of
combat as George mocks their manner and further competition
ensues between the older couple. (Nick and Honey are to be both
audience and participants in this bizarre Sunday-morning ritual.)
George takes advantage of his junior colleague's lack of critical
artistic vocabulary and of his unsureness in strange surround-
ings. The hosts' conversation is barbed but funny and, as much
drink is consumed, a kind of second party atmosphere is established. Honey joins in when Martha provides another performance of her song.

The guests try to ingratiate themselves by praising Martha's
father, the university president. However, George is sarcastic
about the man's virtues – because (as we later see) he and his
father-in-law have a history of disagreement. At this point Martha takes Honey on a tour of the house and George reminds her
not to discuss 'you-know-what' – i.e. their imaginary child. Martha insists that she will do as she pleases.

door-bell chimes This has a significance which goes beyond the usual
   function of the stage device: it registers another phase of ritual.
the bit The character and history of their child. *Note:* 'bit' is a technical
   term for a piece of stage business.
to cover To make up for her outburst which the guests have overheard.
furniture floor Notice the way in which George elaborates upon
   Martha's more staccato pronouncements. This is a pattern followed
   throughout the play.
swinging on Turning forcefully upon.
A quiet intensity? . . . a certain noisy relaxed quality, maybe? The
   technique of presenting opposites for approval by another person is
   perhaps imitated from the teasing of Polonius in Shakespeare's play
   Hamlet, III.2.
joshed Teased or ridiculed.
Never mix . . . Rubbing alcohol Honey's cliché (and Martha's echoing

of the phrase) launches George on a discussion of his wife's extreme drinking habits.

brandy Alexanders . . . things Powerful and/or exotic cocktails.

For the mind's blind eye . . . liver's craw Brain, heart and liver were the rulers of the three parts of the body in Medieval and Renaissance science. They were respectively the seats of thought, emotion and passion. George's salute to the function of liquor has a Shakespearian ring, although this is not a direct quotation. 'Craw' here probably means 'craving'.

Dylan-Thomas-y Richly poetic, sonorous, as in the work of Dylan Thomas, the Welsh poet (1914–53).

Who's afraid . . . See note on page 11.

demurely Modestly, coyly. George is being sarcastic.

sacrifice . . . a more private portion The notion of sacrifice in marriage or sexual relationships ties in with other ritual elements in the play (see sections on Themes and Structure). Taken negatively, George's remark could refer to the emotional castration of men by women.

show me where the . . . Honey's hesitancy in referring to the toilet by name is indicative of her nervous, withdrawn personality.

euphemism The substitution of an agreeable or inoffensive word for one that may seem unpleasant. Instead of using a euphemism, George names the rhetorical term itself. This is a good example of his witty, intellectual manner.

Act One (pages 25-32)

Left on their own, the men talk about academic and other related matters. George puts the younger man through his paces, disarming him somewhat by a revelation of personal details. He explains that he does not run the History Department and implies that this is a disappointment to Martha's father. He also begins to challenge Nick's supposed allegiance to the principles of science – an issue which is to become more prominent (see pages 43-44 and 73-74). Significantly, this is touched off by George asking whether Nick has any children; when the latter says no, George speaks of his fear that biologists wish to make artificial babies. Nick is told that it is for him to find out whether George and Martha have any children. What seems to be a mere conversational gambit is, on a deeper level, a formal challenge. The counter-positions of the two men should now be plain to the audience: the historian, cynical about worldly achievement but still intellectually idealistic; and the biologist, hopeful about advancing his career but lacking in poise and imagination.

Parnassus A mountain in Greece sacred to Apollo and the muses –

hence the source of poetic inspiration. George is referring to the house of his father-in-law (the seat of power in the university). Nick does not understand the allusion.

looking about the room The literally minded Nick misunderstands the drift of George's remarks.

declension A falling off; hence (in grammar) a list of the forms or cases of a word. George humorously suggests that 'bested' is the stage beyond 'best', which is, rightly, the superlative of 'good'.

game Apart from the title description of Act One, this is the first mention of the play's main structural device.

musical beds The sexual equivalent of the game musical chairs; hence moving from partner to partner. George is (intentionally or not) laying the ground for the game 'Hump the Hostess' in Act Two.

Your . . . wife . . . weighs . . . ? Again Nick is slow on the uptake, although George does not provide a pause to signal the change of direction.

Math Department The mistake seems almost deliberate. Whatever his state of awareness, George is intent on puncturing the scientist's mastery of knowledge.

abmaphid George pokes fun at the phenomenon of the super-academic. On the one hand, the acquisition of several degrees can cause mental stress; on the other, it is the means to rise in the university world.

a great deal more . . . disappointing George moves from an assault on genetic engineering to a confession of his own (partial) sense of failure in not reaching the top in the History Department. This marks an adjustment towards Nick, in that personal confidences are allowable in the 'game'.

That's New England . . . This part of the U.S. has a more staid and rarified character than other sections of the country. George implies that nothing changes in an area bound by tradition.

Illyria An ancient name for the area of the Balkans now called Yugoslavia; it had exotic, idyllic connotations and Shakespeare set his play *Twelfth Night* there.

Penguin Island A wild rocky island off the north-east coast of Newfoundland; it was 'discovered' by European adventurers in the sixteenth century. There may be an allusion here to Anatole France's satirical novel *Penguin Island* (1908).

Gomorrah The evil city in Palestine near which, according to Genesis 19,26, Lot's wife was turned to a pillar of salt.

New Carthage Carthage (meaning 'New City') was a famous city of the ancient world, situated on the north African coast. According to legend, it was founded by Dido, the scheming, passionate woman whose tragic affair with Aeneas is related in Virgil's *Aeneid*. Historically, the city became a rival power of Rome (see below under 'Punic Wars'). At a later point St Augustine called Carthage 'a cauldron of unholy loves'. These sex and power associations fit in with the New England society which Albee depicts.

It isn't . . . George compares his college with some famous centres of education.

M.I.T. Massachusetts Institute of Technology (on the east coast).
U.C.L.A. University of California, Los Angeles (on the west coast).
the Sorbonne The oldest part of the university of Paris.
Moscow U. The University of Moscow.
don't you let that get bandied about i.e. that Nick might seek to better his career by moving on to a more renowned university.
Micronesian tortoises Giant tortoises are popularly supposed to have an almost unlimited life span; they are also creatures of fixed habit.

Act One (pages 32-40)

Honey re-enters, saying that Martha is changing her dress. She reveals casually that she knows George and Martha have a son who is to be twenty-one tomorrow. Nick is triumphant: the little secret has been revealed upstairs. George is stunned. Martha has for the first time communicated their fantasy to an outside party. Of course, the audience at this point does not know that the boy is a fiction, despite a few clues. Martha's action is a step beyond sanity but it is also a calculated move to hurt her husband. George manages to control his anger and waits for the opportunity to gain revenge. The guests talk of leaving but their host insists that they stay: if Martha is changing, they are being given a special honour.

When Martha appears, dressed provocatively, she starts praising Nick's achievements and running down her husband's record. George, in the face of this criticism, refuses to light his wife's cigarette. Martha's admiration for Nick's athletic prowess now moves into a phase of flirtation. Learning that Nick was a boxing champion, she recalls her own boxing match with George, mention of which causes him to leave the room. Martha explains how during the war her father wanted the men at the university to learn self-defence; that George refused to box with the president in the garden; upon which she put the gloves on and surprised her husband from behind, knocking him into a huckleberry bush.

Martha says that the incident influenced their whole relationship. Presumably the boxing triumph, accidental though it was, established her supremacy, or at least her surface control of the marriage. George's defeat in the 'game' must have reinforced his lack of traditional male aggression; it symbolized his failure to live up to his father-in-law's expectations.

right ball i.e. testicle. There is a glance here at Martha's role in the household as well as her 'lofty' family connexion. She 'wears the pants'.

Nevertheless, when she enter on page 35 she is described as looking
'voluptuous'.

Sunday chapel dress George is being sarcastic. The dress is probably
an evening one which is décolleté.

barie-poo bar. The use of such baby-language is crucial to the mutual
dependency of George and Martha.

Masters A master's degree (probably master of science).

A.G.D. swamp A goddamn swamp.

the old evolutionary ladder George uses his rival's terms of reference.
Darwinian ideas (e.g. the survival of the fittest) are increasingly
relevant in this game situation.

I will not light your cigarette A small but decisive move in the game
and one which encourages Martha in her antagonism.

intercollegiate ... champion champion of the league through which
matches are played between colleges.

narcissistic Bound up with himself, taking pleasure in his own
attributes.

Would you like to take a walk George counters Martha's flirtation with
Nick by a move towards greater intimacy with Honey. However, it is
not a serious act of seduction.

huckleberry bush A North American shrub similar to whortle-berry or
bilberry (plants which have ritual associations).

Act One (pages 40-51)

George now obtains revenge for the assault upon his character
and reputation. Coming up from behind, he stages a replay of
the wartime match, aiming a convincingly realistic shotgun at
the back of Martha's head. The trick weapon is an effective
theatrical device which breaks the mounting tension and propels
the action towards another climax. Martha participates fully in
the joke and compliments her husband on his resourcefulness;
we catch a glimpse of the love to which her spitefulness is allied.
However, the incident has darker undertones since it prefigures
George's attack on Martha's motherhood and his own story
about the boy who killed his mother with a shotgun (page 61).

George consents to kiss Martha but when she puts his hand on
her breast he rejects any further involvement – ostensibly
because guests are present but also because it puts her in a weak
position. Feeling mocked, Martha returns to the business of
comparing men: she approves the earthiness of Nick's biology
discipline, compared with the more remote world of history.
George responds by expanding on his previous argument that
modern science is reducing the richness and variety of life. (It is
worth noting that Albee was unhappy with the removal of this

discussion from the film version of *Virginia Woolf*; it is an important part of the play.) George does not want the order and constancy which is typified by Nick, the perfect specimen of manly vigour. There is humour when Honey – whether from drunkenness or naiveté – takes George's comments at face value. Nick, for his part, realizes that the rhetorical generalizations belong to a game; yet he is offended by George's assumption that any biology instructor is part of a conspiracy to diminish the quality of life.

Honey now returns to the subject of the absent son by asking when the boy is coming home. Martha tries to stop further discussion of the matter but George will not let his wife off the hook. Stuck with this theme, she manages to score a point against George by attributing his disrespect for the child to doubt as to whether he is its father. The couple then argue about the colour of the boy's eyes – a debate which leads George to attack Martha's father, whom he describes as a great white mouse with beady red eyes.

blue games Indecent or obscene ones.

Pyrrhic victory A victory won at too great a cost.

You don't need any props The phallic implications of George's use of a shotgun are brought out by Martha as she compares Nick's innate 'parts' with her husband's fake gun.

ABSTRUSE!...recondite Martha shows that she is no ignoramus when it comes to vocabulary.

the *meat* of things This echoes the interest which Martha has begun to take in Nick's body.

monoliths Rigidly ordered states or leaders of large, inflexible societies.

chromosomological An elongated form (because part of a rhetorical speech) of the usual adjective 'chromosomal'.

around her things i.e. breasts (as a primitive might do).

you old floozie! Beneath the joke there may be a jibe at George's supposed lack of masculine authority.

Your eyes are...brown Nick the biologist looks for factual detail after Martha's flight of fancy.

Act One (pages 51-57)

While George is getting more drink, Martha explains how she came to marry him. After an affair with a gardener's boy which her father terminated, she got the idea of marrying a university man – someone who could be an appropriate successor to 'Daddy'. As George re-enters, Martha is describing how she fell for the young, alert newcomer to the History Department.

Initially George seems not to mind the story of their courtship being told; He even adds a few details. However, when Martha goes on to expose his failure to live up to early promise – specifically his lack of the qualities necessary for running a college – George is angry and hurt. He asks his wife not to proceed and, when she continues, he smashes a bottle against the portable bar. She taunts him further about his low salary, his lack of personality and his introversion: he was a disappointment to her father because he didn't have the guts to succeed in university affairs. George tries to drown this criticism by singing the 'Virginia Woolf' song and Honey joins in drunkenly. Act One ends with Honey rushing out to be sick and Nick and Martha going to her assistance. George is left along on the stage, a dejected, beaten figure. He has been the main victim in this first series of games, and he is to be humiliated more in Act Two.

the albatross Something that makes accomplishment difficult. In S. T. Coleridge's poem *The Ancient Mariner* (1798) the albatross, a rare bird whose appearance at sea should bring good luck, is shot down and turned into a symbol of doom. Not until the mariner experiences pain and pity can relief occur. There may be an ironic parallel with George's and Martha's relationship. However, her point is simply that – in her father's view – she was not the prize by which a conqueror had access to the top job at the university; at least, this was not his initial opinion. Note the image of the romance or mythic quest, with its overtones of games activity.

along came George This phrase emphasizes the fable-type aspects of the narrative.

howl and claw at the turf This detail also adds to the mythical or fabulous qualities of George's and Martha's courtship, as retold here. Typically in Albee, the bizarre is grounded in observable behaviour.

the other business i.e. George's failure to take over the History Department and the reasons for it. Although George has discussed the matter briefly with Nick (pages 29-30) he cannot bear to have it recited in public.

Revision questions on Act One

1 Which games are played in Act One and what relation do they have to the marital circumstances of George and Martha?

2 Discuss the function of comedy in this act.

3 Compare the behaviour of the two couples.

4 Examine the conflict between the disciplines of History and Biology, as formulated by George.

5 How is the theme of the son developed in this act?

Act Two: Walpurgisnacht (pages 58-74)

The title of this act indicates that the party manoeuvres are moving into a darker phase of ritual: it is the time of witch orgies and mischief; and it is the time when fires are kindled to drive them away.

Nick has returned and the two men are alone on the stage. After more verbal sparring, George's assaults are toned down so that an exchange of attitudes and experience is possible. Nick wonders why Martha and George need an audience for their bouts of 'flagellation', but he admits that their performance is 'impressive'. George inquires about Honey's health and Nick (perhaps because of the drink) relaxes his guard, revealing that he married Honey because he thought she was pregnant. Later this turned out to have been a false alarm. Pouring another bourbon for Nick and musing about parentage, George tells how, as a sixteen-year-old, he went to a bar during the Prohibition era. One of the group he was with caused endless laughter by ordering 'bergin' (a non-existent drink). This boy had shot his own mother accidentally, and the year after he killed his father, again by mistake, in a car-crash. As a result he was thrown into such fits of laughter that he had to be confined to an asylum, from which he has not emerged in thirty years. He has been silent all that time. George's story is followed by a long stage silence. Its fable-like details, such as the porcupine, create a resonance of tragic absurdity in the spectator's mind. And indeed, these events do receive further definition.

The men continue to swap anecdotes and a sort of trust is established, although the two are at times trapped in their separate alcoholic zones. There is an amusing sequence where George carries on discussing his marriage while Nick is beginning to describe his own — a characteristic structural overlap in this play. George scores a bull's-eye when he suggests that Nick married Honey for her money: it transpires that her father made a fortune out of religion by somewhat devious means, and that this made the alliance to Honey tolerable. George draws a parallel with the wealth which Martha's father inherited — or perhaps milked from the university (we are not sure what to believe here). Nick is encouraged to express more of his character and, with a mixture of joky exhibitionism and crude voracity, he says that he will gain promotion by sleeping with influential university wives – including Martha. When George tries to explain the shallowness of such success, Nick dismisses his advice with a laugh. But the history professor is serious and he delivers a long speech in favour of civilized values against mere brutishness.

Walpurgisnacht Walpurgis Night, the eve of May Day, when witches are most powerful: they are supposed to speed through the air on their hellish business. At the same time, people in Central Europe used to prepare for the expulsion of these evil powers on the day following. This would involve ceremonial burning of bundles of twigs, the ringing of bells and banging of pots, and the shouting of a special chant.

She doesn't . . . rest home i.e. Martha does not take time off to relax.

flagellation Deriving pleasure or satisfaction from beating oneself or another – originally a public act of penance or punishment.

hysterical pregnancy A mentally induced condition marked by many of the symptoms of pregnancy.

the Punic Wars Between the Romans and the Carthaginians (in three phases from 265 to 146 B.C.). George may be joking about his age as well as making an apt reference to the preparation for his present place of employment.

gin mill Bar, saloon.

Prohibition The period from 1920 to 1933 when the manufacture and sale of alcoholic liquor was forbidden in the United States.

bergin A malapropism for Bourbon. Presumably the boy has conflated Bourbon whiskey and Burgundy wine.

pep-talker One who argues forcefully in order to arouse enthusiasm for an idea or course of action.

a bean bag A small bag of dried beans, used in games. Another explicit reference to a ritual.

Cyclops One of a race of giants in Greek mythology; they had only one eye in the middle of the forehead.

Monstre! Monster. (Fr.) George starts speaking in French and Martha follows.

Cochon! Pig (Fr.)

Bête Beast. (Fr.)

Canaille! Scoundrel. (Fr.)

Putain! Prostitute. (Fr.)

play . . . doctor Note the reference to a childhood game.

In *spite* of what they say about Chinese women Far Eastern women have a reputation for being more solicitous of their partner's satisfaction than Western women. Nick does not understand.

cretins A rather feeble pun on Cretans.

outhouses Outside lavatories.

she married the white mouse Note the continuing fable-like qualities of the narrative.

peach pie i.e. a sweet thing to devour.

get the goods i.e. the low-down or essential information.

Unh-unh. *You've* got history . . . Nick plays the literalist, as we have been led to expect.

pertinent Relevant to his promotion because of their connexions.

The way to a man's heart . . . wife's belly A clever play on the usual idea that food is the key to a man's heart.

Act Two (page 74-84)

Martha and Honey re-enter, the latter still in a delicate state. Immediately there is another argument between the hosts, this time over the cause of Honey's sickness. Honey herself tries to defuse the situation, saying that her nausea is habitual. Martha then accuses George of making their son sick and he retaliates by suggesting that it was Martha's unnatural physical interest in the boy which made him throw up and run away from home.

A key moment now occurs when Martha reveals in passing that George used to drink 'bergin'. This links up with the story which George has told Nick. It is improbable that we are meant to believe that George killed his parents too as this aspect of his character is undeveloped. More likely there is some tragedy or failure in his family history which he has transformed into a fable. He is, after all, an aspiring novelist. The truth of the story probably relates to George's mental state rather than to any literal event. Drama can get away with such 'distant' or symbolic effects because the theatre audience cannot stop to investigate but must follow the action forward.

With a deft sense of what will hurt George most, Martha brings up the subject of his book, which her father would not let George publish. This is another topic that George does not want discussed in front of strangers. For any writer their work is sacrosanct but in this case something more than pride is at stake. Martha's scorn for her husband's writing is enacted in an increasingly sensational way – for she starts dancing close to Nick, speaking in rhymes to the pulse of the music. As Richard Amacher has pointed out, the transition from a verbal reference (page 77) to actual dancing shows how Albee can, 'in the seemingly static situation of the play, introduce considerable variety and movement.'

Martha explains how George's novel was suppressed because it dealt with unseemly matters – the 'bergin' story which he has related to Nick – and that George defended the book's integrity by confessing that it was based on his own experience. Up to this point George has just managed to keep his cool; however, when his verbal pleas fail to prevent Martha from going on, he grabs her by the throat, saying that he will kill her. There is a struggle in which Nick tears George from Martha and throws him to the floor. This physical combat marks a shift in atmosphere: the game-playing has become a matter of life and death – if not literally, at least symbolically. The characters are fighting to retain their identity.

Like Big Ben i.e. like clockwork (or for ages).
something having clicked Nick begins to suspect that the bergin boy was George.
Oh, I love dancing Honey interprets George's metaphor literally.
hit the sack Usually 'go to bed'. Here the prelude (dancing) is indicated.
Second movement, Beethoven's 7th Symphony George's choice is (intentionally) inappropriate for dancing.
I thought it was fitting From one point of view, George's selection matches the heavy ritual of the scene.
Sacre du Printemps Stravinsky's 'The Rite of Spring', a composition which portrays fertility and sacrificial ritual.
consciously making rhymed speech Another ritual element, although on the surface it is done merely to impress or raise a laugh.

Act Two (page 84–96)

After the tussle the characters eye each other warily. George is the first to initiate other business: having been the victim, he establishes himself as master of ceremonies. He formalizes the events of Act Two by naming each game – 'Humiliate the Host', 'Get the Guests' and 'Hump the Hostess'. The first game, he says, has been played out; now it is time to engage in the second one. He wants revenge for the way in which Nick has participated in Martha's attack on his manhood, his art and his outlook. The young couple must pay a price for their audience or active role in the dismantling of George's personality.

We are, of course, intrigued by this turnaround in the balance of power. It happens on a verbal level – appropriate after the violence of the throttling episode. George begins in a subdued tone but builds up to another climax. His strategy is to narrate the plot of what he claims is his second novel; in fact the story is an ironic reworking of the details of Nick's and Honey's marriage, as related to George by Nick at the beginning of this act. George gives the story an allegorical feel, so that the direct personal references are clothed in generality. Nick realizes what is happening and tries to stop the narration in mid-flow, but George insists on finishing his tale. Ironically, Honey asks that George be allowed to go on. She is too polite and slow-witted to see George's darker purpose until he gets to the hysterical pregnancy – at which point she perceives that Nick has given their most intimate secret away. She runs out in a state of shock.

Nick reprimands George for the demolition of Honey and for the betrayal of confidence. Notice how he places his main emphasis on the hurt that he has suffered. He says that he will exact vengeance in due course, playing George's language (i.e. he will act out an extreme role). There is now an interlude during which George and Martha assess the evening's events and the nature of their relationship. George expects Martha to have appreciated the display of savagery but she claims that his behaviour makes her sick. She says that their marriage, which she calls an 'arrangement', has finally snapped'. ('Snap' is a key word in this play – see the section on Style.) Almost immediately the tension rises again as they declare total war on each other.

True or false? A games catch phrase which in this context has deeper associations concerning illusion and reality.

Blondie and his frau out of the plain states came A parody of the English poet Robert Browning's 'Childe Roland to the Dark Tower Came' (1852). This narrative monologue describes a quest through a barren landscape for the mysterious dark tower, which symbolizes recognition of self, or possibly death. There is a clear link with the themes of Albee's play.

pan-Kansas swimming champeen Swimming champion of the whole of Kansas.

in the upchuck In the toilet (i.e. vomiting).

swine...truffles Pigs or dogs are trained to sniff out and uproot truffles (underground fungi considered to be delicacies).

pigmy hunting Either 'picking on smaller creatures' or 'tracking down the bizarre' (probably the former).

melons i.e. breasts.

underneath the barnacles i.e. under the rough hard shell.

Act Two (pages 96-108)

We move on now to the third game, 'Hump the Hostess', which involves even more sensational behaviour. Albee has made this credible by showing Nick and Martha growing closer (from the rapport established on page 38 to the dancing on pages 80-82). While George is out getting ice, Martha begins to seduce Nick, slipping her hand between his legs. Their sex play is well advanced by the time George returns. His reaction is to pretend not to notice – or be concerned by – Martha's bold demonstration of infidelity. Instead he talks in a cheerful tone and sits down to read a book, facing away from the other two. This show of indifference is calculated to enrage Martha, for she has hoped to make George jealous. Unable to stir George with the reminder that she is necking with her guest, Martha leads Nick into the kitchen. (Perhaps it is only now that she decides to go all the way with him.)

George is left alone on the stage reading his book, which turns out to be Spengler's *Decline of the West* – a work that bears upon his domestic situation. He releases his frustration by hurling the book at the door chimes, which then ring loudly. This wakes Honey, who returns from her foetal repose on the bathroom floor. George finds her naiveté infuriating and tries to explain what is really going on – specifically what her husband and Martha are doing in the kitchen. Meanwhile, Honey, who is still in a daze, discloses her big secret: that she is afraid of having children. George immediately grasps that her headaches and sickness stem from the pills which she takes to avoid pregnancy – and that Nick does not know.

Albee has constructed this scene carefully so that the actions of the two unmarried couples are balanced: as we hear laughter and the crash of dishes from off-stage (signs of 'humping'), the talk on stage is of generation and the obliteration of life. When Honey asks who rang the bell, George assumes she is referring to the game in the next room, but he soon understands her more literal drift. Mention of the chimes provides him with an idea for the ultimate defeat of Martha: he pretends that a message has been delivered announcing the death of their son. Honey is shocked further and the act ends with George rehearsing his grim news.

What appears to be cruelty may yet become an instrument of compassion: George's laughter is mixed with tears, indicating that he bemoans the loss of Martha. He has suffered hideously during the witches' festival as infernal rites are enacted. He has been driven to deeds of spite and malice. Nevertheless, as Anna Paolucci has remarked, George 'with characteristic resiliency . . . manages to turn chaos into meaningful reality.' Albee's feat in rendering these extremes of behaviour credible is remarkable. He has pulled a primitive ritual into the second half of the twentieth century and made the structure seamless: we never feel that we are out of an east coast university house, whatever abnormalities occur.

Mugging Grimacing.

all in the faculty A play on the phrase 'all in the family'.

ice for the lamps of China, Manchuria thrown in George brings ice to cool down (refresh or extinguish) dangerously heated emotion. Manchuria, a region in north-east China, indicates vastness of space.

Easy Street A situation without financial worries.

hootch up Refill (glass) with alcohol.

worm turns? . . . straight line Martha argues that George is like a worm in one respect but not in another: he moves low and in a straight line but he does not turn – i.e. change.

he hasn't seen it This is ambiguous: either her vagina or her performance routine. The drift in each case is similar. George matches (and exceeds) the others' vulgarity.

footwork Literally the use of the feet, as in games (especially boxing). George means 'preliminary or peripheral manoeuvres'.

'And the west . . .' A quotation from or paraphrase of Oswald Spengler's *The Decline of the West* (1918), the great German philosophical work which challenged the notion of history as progress.

Poe-bells The chimes remind Honey of the famous poem 'The Bells' by Edgar Allan Poe (1809-1849). Significantly, Poe's bells are said to keep time 'In a sort of Runic rhyme'.

dry run for the wave of the future For George, Nick's and Martha's (supposed) copulation represents a prefigurement of the mechanistic creation of more perfect beings.

BANG! George plays on the word's dual meaning: firstly to make a loud sound and secondly to have sexual intercourse.

Revision questions on Act Two

1 Do you think that the three games make good theatre? Examine language and action.

2 Do you think that George's 'bergin' tale is autobiographical? (Remember Martha's comment at the top of page 93).

3 Why does Albee leave the reader to form his own opinion of the story's status and relevance?

4 Why is George so cruel to Honey in this act?

5 Do you find the behaviour of Martha and Nick credible?

Act Three: The Exorcism (pages 109-115)

The ritual framework of the play demands that, after the climax of black festivity, evil should be driven out (i.e. exorcized). A

blasphemous parody of the Mass was supposed to have been
enacted at the witches' sabbath. In addition, the fat of murdered
unbaptized infants was used by the witches as an ointment to confer
special power, such as the means to fly. Albee takes these two
elements and transfers them to the purifying ritual – a move which
helps to link the processes of destruction and re-creation. Nick's
'copulation' with Martha, incidentally, is a dim echo of the tradition
that the devil was supposed to have had sexual intercourse with the
witches during the festival. As Richard Amacher has observed, the
spirits which have to be driven out in *Virginia Woolf* are not so much
personages as subconscious forces, such as jealousy and pride,
which poison the marriage relationship. George's and Martha's
child *is* a human figure but ultimately he proves to be a figment of
the imagination.

The last act presents two more games: 'Houseboy' and 'Bringing
up Baby'. The first of these is not named in George's scheme but on
page 119 he speaks of it as part of a game. Again Albee manages to
vary the mood in an effective way, keeping the audience interested
and pushing the action on to an emotionally satisfying close.

Martha has a long opening monologue – one of those 'arias'
characteristic of Albee – in which she reveals her inner feelings after
all the posturing. This is not so much her real (i.e. only) self as
another, more tender part of her character. She sings to herself in a
drunken haze and – between bursts of laughter – reflects upon the
misery of life. Her thoughts turn upon George in a more kindly
manner. When Nick reappears, it become evident that he has failed
to make love to Martha, no doubt because of over-consumption of
alcohol. Martha complains about his performance and reflects that
there is only one man who has ever made her happy. Nick cannot
believe that this is George, but Martha does mean him – in this
moment of enlightenment. The mutual interdependence of
George and Martha comes suddenly into focus, as she speaks
lovingly of his concern for her. She shows how much she values his
tolerance and wit, as well as his ability to keep learning new games.
Nick is puzzled and Martha pours scorn on his limited, scientific
consciousness. She demands that he play the role of houseboy, as a
penalty for failing to satisfy her sexually. This new game is set off by
the ringing of the door chimes.

Drop me . . . shoe Martha recites part of a song – probably the chorus. She
may be ad-libbing or remembering an old hit. We see the softer side of her
performance routine.
vices A play on 'devices'.

we take our tears . . . drinks The ritualistic function of the drinking sessions is emphasized.

songwriter Martha refers to her line 'I've got windshield . . . you' but the remark could be applied more generally. She, as well as her husband, is a phrasemaker.

the can The toilet (U.S.).

'tis the refuge we take . . . Martha affects a poetic, philosophical tone.

I am the Earth Mother Martha functions in this ritual as the female spirit of fertility. There are, however, ironies attached to the role.

lunk-heads Dull-witted people.

goo-goo Loving, enticing.

You see all the little specs . . . goes on Martha now takes a similar line to George in criticizing the limitations of empirical science.

makes like Plays the part of, acts like.

gattling gun An early machine gun, the sound of which Martha now proceeds to imitate.

Can't you get the latch up, either? A reference to Nick's recent sexual impotence.

houseboy A person who performs general work around the house.

flunky Footman, person performing menial duties.

'Just a gigolo . . .' A song by Irving Caesar and Leonello Casucci from the musical film *Lover Come Back* (1946), starring Lucille Ball. (A gigolo is a young man supported by an older woman, often in return for sexual favours.) This is a further insult to Nick.

Act Three (pages 115-123)

When Nick opens the door – echoing George's role at the beginning of the play – a huge bunch of snapdragons is thrust in and a falsetto voice chants a Spanish funeral-refrain. Like the shotgun in Act One, this is an expressionist device, reminiscent of Strindberg, Artaud and certain German painters. (Expressionism is the active projection of inner concerns, often in uncompromisingly pure images and bright colours.) Behind the flowers, of course, is George. The bouquet is one of the most stunning effects in the play – at once amusing and grotesque. The snapdragons have symbolic overtones (life-bestowing or removing); they pick up on Martha's use of the word 'snap' (pages 94-95) and anticipate George's remarks on pages 120 and 124.

George steps into the room and pretends to take Nick for his returned son. Nick retreats, intimating that he wishes to leave. Martha, however, commands him to remain in his role as houseboy. The hosts do a little comedy routine on the theme of 'houseboy'. This leads into an important dialogue in which

George and Martha debate the realism of their stories – specifically, whether George went to the Mediterranean as he now says
he did. Nick breaks in with a question about the parents whom
George is supposed to have killed. After a telling pause Martha
and George give different answers, and the latter suggests that
there is no objective reality in life.

Martha has earlier revealed that Nick did not make it with her
but, pressed by Nick's demand to be released from his role as
houseboy, she implies that he did perform the full act. George,
not knowing what to believe, throws the snapdragons one by one
at Martha and Nick, as if they were spears. While he does this,
George chants 'SNAP ... SNAP'. This is a ritualized act of
aggression and another theatrically impressive performance.
George has, in fact, come as a 'dragon-slayer', a champion who
will rid the company of its problem-spirit. Shortly before this
George has said or sung 'Here we go round the mulberry bush'
(page 119). Margaret Murray in *The God of the Witches* suggests
that the round dance, which survives in children's games, may
have its origin in dances performed at the witches' sabbath. Thus
the world of magic transformation is kept before us, through
verbal hints and visual details.

George says that there is one more game to play, called 'Bringing up Baby', but for this everyone must be present. Nick is sent to
retrieve Honey from the bathroom. Martha is at first reluctant to
engage in further games activity; perhaps she senses from her
husband's enthusiasm that her undiminished power is about to be
taken away. (Of the four contestants, Martha alone is unhurt, or
virtually so, up to this point.) Eventually George arouses his wife's
combative instincts and they agree to fight 'to the death'.

Flores: flores para los muertos Flowers for the dead. This is a refrain
from Tennessee Williams' *A Streetcar Named Desire* (1947), a play which
as a study of psychological extremes has something in common with
Virginia Woolf.

Chippie-chippie... Acting in an impudent, lively way.

I brung ya George affects a brogue, emphasizing the absurd nature of
his role.

Violence! A play on or mistake for 'Violets'. The word is appropriate
thematically.

I'm nobody's houseboy now 'Nobody's Sweetheart Now' is a song by
Gus Kahn and others from the musical film *I'm Nobody's Sweetheart Now*
(1940). It also featured in the Doris Day film *I'll See You in My Dreams*
(1951).

Chastity Diana, the moon-goddess, is, in one of her aspects, patroness of chastity. George may be alluding to the failure of Nick's and Martha's sex-act, and/or to the paradox by which Diana is both goddess of fertility and of chastity.

it came back up George's interpretation of nature and the cosmos is poetic or imaginative rather than scientific. This accords with his previous arguments.

You don't make it ... houseboy Again the games dimension is emphasized.

Here we go ... mulberry bush This relates to the tune of the 'Virginia Woolf' song but it may also echo the huckleberry bush incident. 'Here We Go Round The Mulberry Bush' appeared in *Mother Goose's Melodies* (1765). The tune was taken from a song called 'Nancy Dawson', about a celebrated dancer in the reign of George II. The rhyme goes:
'Here we go round the mulberry bush,
The mulberry bush, the mulberry bush,
Here we go round the mulberry bush
On a cold and frosty morning.'
Successive verses introduce other actions which the children can do as they sing and dance (e.g. washing hands).

snap go the dragons A play on 'Pop Goes the Weasel'.

plough Perhaps 'sexual organ'. Or else the whole phrase could mean 'Go back to the farm' (addressed to a virile but lowly person).

blue-veined Aristocratic (i.e. because she is the daughter of the college president).

the little dip A simpleton, a person who is mentally unbalanced.

an Easter pageant i.e. an innocent entertainment.

slugging Striking heavily (as in a boxing match) or walking doggedly.

Act Three (pages 123-139)

Nick re-enters with Honey and the last phase begins. George insists that they all sit down because this is to be a civilized game. But Honey's reference to her game of peeling the labels off brandy bottles sets George off on a long account of progressive truth-finding. He says that the final stage is when you arrive at the marrow inside the bone – an image which sounds ominous. He then insists that the time has come for a full account of his and Martha's son. He repeats his assertion that Martha took an erotic interest in the boy, and, after an attempt to stop the narration, she launches into her own version of the son's upbringing. George is a kind of stage director here, coaxing his wife through a familiar routine. The two have different ideas about the boy's physical appearance but they manage to construct a solid enough picture. We gain further insight into the softer, dreamier (and sentimental) side of Martha's character. George too is seen in a more pleasant frame of mind. In fact, the theatrical urge which has been so destructive hitherto begins to assume a healthier aspect.

Just as Martha climbs up to a more idealized level of reminiscence, George starts punctuating her comments with phrases from the Requiem Mass. This produces a duet effect, similar to that at the end of Act One but less jarring in tone. George now takes on the role of high priest, blessing his wife's recital. For the moment the death associations are submerged. The action hovers between absurdity and profound mystery. Honey is sufficiently moved to exclaim suddenly that she wants a child. This major development is not given much attention by Martha, who is self-absorbed. Having completed her rapturous description, she cannot resist a dig at George: she says that such perfection could not endure with him around. In her present mood, she does not want to be overly critical, but George will not let her retreat now that battle territory has been reached. He accuses Martha of using the son as a weapon against him. She in turn claims that the boy could not come to terms with his father's failure. The quarrel reaches a climax with the duet on page 132-33, during which Martha asserts that her child is the one thing which she has held dear in a sordid marriage. As a background to this protest, George intones the *Libera me*, a liturgical response about the day of judgement. The duet is a good example of the sculptural quality of Albee's writing: words take on a physical aspect in space.

Nick and Honey want the game to end here but George persists in drawing it out. Honey gets increasingly desperate as George proceeds to tell Martha about the death of their son – announced in a telegram which he has since eaten. The account is tragicomic, taking in details from elsewhere, such as the car accident and the porcupine. In a consummate rhetorical flourish, George has turned the child game full-circle, leaving Martha with no opportunity to re-create the myth. She complains that George cannot decide to kill the boy of his own accord, and she leaps wildly at him. However, as George reminds her, the two had an understanding that they would not share their dream with anyone else. Martha, in breaking that agreement, has brought the 'tragedy' upon herself.

Despite what they have witnessed earlier, Nick and Honey are genuinely concerned for Martha's welfare. They treat the death seriously, even as one of them – Nick – realizes that the 'son' story has been a fantasy. He encourages George and Martha to reveal the truth: that they could not have children. Albee's stage direction ('a hint of communion') indicates how far the mood has progressed from the jokes and bitterness of the previous acts. Martha and George have been brought closer by the explosion of their private myth. As dawn is about to break, Nick and Honey leave the house, also wiser in their way for what they have experienced.

Hip, hop ... you a bunny Nick and Honey now do their version of child-talk.

I don't remember ... Honey tries to persuade George to desist from revealing the death of the son.

We all peel labels i.e. reveal hidden layers of experience.

Our son was born ... It is evident from this recital that part of the son story has been well rehearsed over the years.

Absolve, Domine, animas ... delictorum Absolve, O Lord, the souls of all the faithful departed from every bond of sin.

Et gratia ... ultionis And by the help of Thy grace, may they be enabled to escape the judgement of vengeance.

Et lucis ... perfrui And enjoy the blessedness of light eternal.

In Paradisum ... Angeli May the Angels lead thee into Paradise.

In memoria ... timebit The just man shall be in everlasting remembrance; he shall not fear the evil hearing.

Dominus vobiscum May the Lord be with you.

Libera me ... ignem Deliver me, O Lord, from everlasting death in that dreadful day when heaven and earth shall quake, when thou shalt come to judge the world by fire. I tremble and am sore afraid, at the judgement and the wrath to come; when heaven and earth shall quake. O that day, that day of wrath, of calamity and woe, a great day and exceeding bitter. When thou shalt come to judge the world by fire. Rest eternal grant unto him, O Lord; and let light perpetual shine upon him. (Then the first sentence is repeated.)

Kyrie ... eleison Lord, have pity, Christ, have pity. Lord, have pity.

a chaw A chew, i.e. a meditative chat.

Oh my God Nick realizes that the details of the son's death are similar (and too coincidental) to those in George's story of the bergin boy (page 62).

I ate it This is a parody of the eating of the host (the round wafer of bread which represents the body of Christ). In killing the child, George makes a symbolic sacrifice. He completes the act, as it were, by swallowing the evidence.

Requiescat in pace May he rest in peace.

Requiem ... Domine Eternal rest give unto them, O Lord.

Et lux ... eis And let perpetual light shine upon them.

Act Three (pages 139-40)

The ending of *Virginia Woolf* has an almost religious feel, as George and Martha face up to what they have been through. Notice how their dialogue is laid out on the page: one word or phrase is allotted to each in sequence, as if the torrent of language has slowed down and they have to learn to speak again. The stage direction emphasizes this softness and slowness of sound. Martha still asks George whether he had to destroy the child and he answers simply that it was time for such a move. He claims that their situation will be better; she says that she is not sure. For a moment Martha seems to suggest resurrecting the boy (or finding another escapist myth), but George firmly denies such a possibility. She leans her head against him like a child as he sings the 'Virginia Woolf' rhyme, and she admits finally that *she* is afraid of Virginia Woolf. With their bodies frozen in this position, the play comes to a close.

Opinions differ about the degree of hope offered by Albee's conclusion. There are signs of a new rapport and commitment between husband and wife. Martha has become a more sympathetic character, one who excites our pity. On the other hand, we cannot be confident that the removal of illusion will lead to any lasting happiness. It is difficult to forget the malicious warring behaviour of the first two and a half acts. Moreover, George and Martha seem isolated and exhausted in their moment of enlightenment.

What is clear is that Albee has constructed the last act so that a change of awareness is possible. Irony is played down and a serious, semi-tragic note is sounded. It is important to remember that both couples undergo a change: Nick and Honey have lived a shallow existence, based on material ambition and mutual deception. Their sugary security has been broken by the games ritual and they have the chance of reconstructing their lives on a surer footing. Nick is less of a cocky, all-American kid, and Honey seems less insipid. As a parallel to Martha's awakening, Honey seems to have overcome her fear of pregnancy. George and Martha have lived a bizarre, over-dramatized existence in which their insufficiencies have been buried beneath layers of gameplaying. Now that their patterns of communication (or noncommunication) have been taken to the limit, a more direct mode of relating to one another is available to them. The fantasy-son has been knocked away like a useless prop. In Martha's admission that she is afraid of Virginia Woolf, there is an answer to the riddle posed at the beginning of the play. She particularly (in her role as the domineering flirtatious wife), and the other characters to a lesser degree, have been afraid of the naked self, the unadorned truth. A time for reassessment has come, if these people can grasp the opportunity offered.

Revision questions on Act Three

1 How far can we sympathize with Martha in this act?

2 One critic complained that Albee dragged the third act out 'to excessive lengths.' Do you think that the author's method is justified and how effective would it be in the theatre? (Bear in mind the pace of the previous acts.)

3 How would you interpret the ending of the play? Do you think that the games between George and Martha are finished?

4 Where do you find a distinct change or changes of tone in this act? Explain Albee's intention here.

5 Give three examples of striking imagery or language used in this act and say why you think they are significant.

Edward Albee's art in *Who's Afraid of Virginia Woolf*
The characters

Martha

Who's Afraid of Viriginia Woolf? . . . I . . . am . . . George

Martha is a recognizable (if exaggerated) type in American society: the aggressive, independent woman. She parades her sexual charms and seeks to control the household, subjecting her husband to continual criticism – especially in front of others. On one level the play's title could be interpreted as 'Who is afraid of Martha?', for she is an intimidating and destructive person. (Virginia Woolf's novel *Between the Acts* contains a Lady Harpy Harraden.) Albee intensifies the negative qualities of the type to such an extent that he has been accused of being a misogynist (i.e. woman-hater). Martha's vulgarity makes her a parody of the Earth Mother, source of fertility, nourishment and protection. The positive attributes of the emancipated female are, in her, turned to vicious egotism and decadence. On the other hand, as 'original game-girl' (page 122) she is a most entertaining figure. Moreover, we are enabled finally to view her problems in a sympathetic light.

The play provides plenty of information about Martha's upbringing and state of mind. In Act One (pages 52–53) we discover that her mother died when she was young and that she grew up with her father. George's account on page 69 adds the detail that Martha's father married again – to a wealthy older woman. (If this is a fiction, it seems to have psychological authenticity.) Martha speaks in glowing terms of the rapport she had with her father but it seems likely that her worship and his fondness (page 52) are the products of delusion and nostalgia. She was, after all, packed off to boarding school, and her father put a swift end to her first serious relationship (with the gardener's boy). The college president does not sound like a warm emotional character, and George is probably speaking the truth when he says (page 131) that Martha's father does not care what happens to his only daughter.

Martha returned from finishing school and used her ladylike graces in caring for her father. In an effort to please him, or at least to fulfil a sense of family destiny, she looked for a husband amongst the university staff. After some years had passed,

George arrived on the scene – young, vigorous, intelligent and unmarried. Martha pitched on him, assuming that he would make his way up the professional ladder and take over as college president. It is common enough for a woman to wish to be married to a status symbol, but Martha's reminiscences suggest strongly that her real motivation was to gain the approval of her father, after years of near-rejection. The 'great white mouse', as George calls him, looms large behind the action. Apparently, he is a powerful and efficient administrator who admires traditional male virtues, such as physical fitness. It would be in keeping with these qualities for him to have always wanted a son and to have made Martha feel second-best. Even if there was affection between father and daughter this could be the case at crucial moments.

George, then, became an image of hope for the woman who lacked a complete role. That he failed to live up to expectations can be explained partly by Martha's own position. She has been well educated (see, for instance, pages 22, 44) but – typically in the period being described – she was not groomed for a public occupation. Her work is confined to domestic chores and entertainment functions. Hence her mental alertness tends to be channelled into petty wrangling and gamesmanship. The American economist J. K. Galbraith observed that Martha is a familiar type on the university scene: 'She is assertive, rowdy and rough-talking . . . she is determined that, while her sex may keep her out of classrooms and faculty meetings, it damn well won't keep her out of conversations and academic politics.' Within the terms of this closed society, Martha can only achieve respect and admiration via her husband's career. When George neglects to pursue worldly ambition, Martha feels humiliated and betrayed. In particular, she fails to measure up to the demands laid down by her father.

Martha's frustrated energy finds an outlet in constant marital bickering, in heavy consumption of alcohol and in sordid love affairs. She refers to the latter as 'crummy, totally pointless infidelities' (page 111); evidently, they leave her dissatisfied. Nick sums up Martha's loud, over-active behaviour when he tells George, in a factual tone, 'She doesn't really spend any time in a rest home' (page 58). Martha's main source of consolation is her fantasy child, which until now has remained a secret between husband and wife. The son is proof of her femininity and he embodies those qualities which George lacks (hence the erotic undertone as she describes his personality and appearance). The idealized male may even be a substitute for the brother she never had, since only by producing a son can Martha fulfil her father's desire to perpetuate the line. When George breaks the illusion he is both revenging himself for years of laceration and releasing Martha from the cul-de-sac of her dreams. It is important to remember that the son myth is a joint creation – an imaginative device for resisting a society which seems to be progressing towards test-tube humanity. Yet it cannot be an adequate substitute for living flesh and blood. The physical contact between George and Martha at the end of the play, tentative though it is, provides a more solid base for life.

For much of the play Martha delights in exposing her husband's inadequacies: his intellectual remoteness, his writing pretensions, his lack of physical vigour and his failure to advance his career. She tortures him mercilessly in front of the guests. Nevertheless, it is clear that they both derive a perverse satisfaction from these blistering bouts. The games are sado-masochistic: that is to say, the participants get pleasure out of inflicting pain on each other. As Martha says to George on page 92, he married her for her strength and wildness. (Obviously he did not marry her to be torn apart and humiliated but there is a certain truth in Martha's comment, especially when we bear in mind the account of their courtship on page 54.) George is weary of the games but he know that there is a certain nobility in playing them out to the finish.

The crucial explanation of George's and Martha's relationship comes on pages 112-114. Nick assumes that because George has had his back broken (symbolically) he does not measure up to Martha's image of manhood. Now, however, Martha praises her husband for his tolerance, his kindness and his understanding. She says that he is the only person who has the agility to follow her games and initiate manoeuvres. Only George, in fact, can make her happy. It is as if a curtain has been pulled aside to reveal the 'plus' factor which has kept the two together for so long.

The third act turns Martha into a much more interesting character. Previously we have seen her as a cruel, selfish manipulator and as a flaunter of over-extended charms. George refers to Martha's continual 'braying', which is an apt description of her aggressive, egotistical manner. Her assaults on George's personality are a painful but also entertaining exaggeration of wifely needling. It is true that she has moments of tenderness and satisfaction (e.g. pages 41–42). But essentially

Martha is a coarse, unpleasant figure up to the end of Act Two. It is a major achievement that Albee manages to arouse compassion for her plight in Act Three. The presentation of her suffering and fear is moving and convincing. Having dominated the other characters for two acts, Martha sinks into a pit where she has to confront her own unhappiness. We get a glimpse of another, more attractive side to her character. This is a neat development in the plot and it makes her a richer, more rounded personality. The insight into her situation surely exonerates Albee from the charge of misrepresenting femininity. If Martha is 'larger than life', she is, finally, a believable and recognizable type in the modern world. The individual portrait immortalizes the type. Although George is in many ways the prime-mover and the speaker of the best lines, it is Martha who is the most memorable character in the play.

George

You never do anything . . . You just sit around and *talk*

Just as Martha exemplifies a certain kind of college personality, George typifies another: that of the teacher who is more interested in his subject than in the business of administration. According to Martha's public statements, George is a failure: he is too 'contemplative' to have bothered with the nitty-gritty of running a university department. Hence he has not progressed up the career ladder (see pages 29-30, 55-57). As his witty conversation makes clear, George is an intellectual who prefers not to wrestle with the shallow satisfactions of student-management. In this anti-practical and anti-go-getting bias, he is contrasted with Nick, the opportunist. George has retreated into a world of scholarship from which he can view events with ironic detachment. On the domestic front, he dispenses drink but does not assert himself in the role of husband. We notice that Martha has invited guests without asking George's opinion. When his wife proceeds to seduce Nick, George settles into reading a book. The emblem of this associate professor's failure is the boxing incident, during which he was humiliated by his wife in front of her father (also his employer). Clearly, as Thomas Porter has remarked, George's 'worth as a person . . . is not dependent on his achievement of status either in the business world or at home.'

In fact, Albee plots the action so as to emphasize George's 'ineffectuality' (page 70) in conventional terms, such as manly power. His weapon is his acute intelligence and his 'long view' of things. Thus, at a certain point, George comes into his own as an agent of salvation. His seeming weakness becomes a form of strength. This development is prepared for by George's verbal agility: both in his oblique wordplay and in his philosophical pronouncements, he undermines the values of the other three inhabitants of New Carthage. Accused of being a failure in the modern world of brisk competition, George questions the terms by which such an assessment is reached. Although he is capable of physical aggression (pages 83-84), he operates mainly through language games and disputes. His dissection of Nick's outlook, from the portrait description (pages 20–21) to the stud image (page 120), is masterly.

George seems to follow Spengler in viewing history as a series of culture cycles in which short periods of creativity and enlightenment are followed by sterility and mechanical behaviour. On three occasions (pages 29–31, 45–47, 73–74) he expresses anxiety about the threat posed by technology. He treats Nick, the biologist, as a representative of the 'progress at any cost' lobby. In particular, he fears that life will become standardized through genetic engineering. He prefers the rich unpredictability of nature. George's obsession with the possible alteration of chromosomes must relate to his and Martha's failure to produce offspring. Nevertheless, the viewpoint is a valid one, treated at greater length by Aldous Huxley in *Brave New World* (1932). When George says that he will not 'give up Berlin' (page 46) he makes a general and a personal point: that his culture should not surrender to the grey conformity of communism and that he would not want to lose the exotic variety of a highly individual city. Fortunately for the play's development and character interest, these serious observations are rendered entertaining though George's manner of delivery. He can inflate his contemplative streak with a nice sense of irony and the ridiculous. In his stream of quips and puns he is a match for Martha and a victor over Nick. Behind the mask of detachment, George knows exactly what is going on.

It is tempting to see George as a mouthpiece for Albee himself, the artist at odds with society's values. However, George is by no means an idealized, heroic figure. His problems and weaknesses are exposed like everyone else's. To a certain extent he is responsible for Martha's present state, in that he has tolerated her selfishness and participated in her fantasy. During the play he is seen to lose his grip on two occasions (pages 56 and

83-84), although such violence should be seen in a performance context. He is extremely cruel to Honey at the end of Act Two. There is also the question of his responsibility for the death of his parents. George's story of the 'bergin' boy who accidentally killed his parents gains more and more autobiographical significance as the play goes on (see, for instance, Martha's comments on pages 83 and 93). Finally George works some of the details into the narrative of sonny-Jim's death (page 135). Does this dual-tragedy explain George's adult withdrawal from business and domestic action? As indicated in the commentary on Act Two, it is preferable to regard the accident story as a symbolic version of George's adolescence, rather than a literal account. There is a kind of truth in the illusion — as with so much else in the George-and-Martha world. What seems certain is that George carries within himself a degree of guilt concerning the welfare of his family. Perhaps he abandoned his parents because he was ashamed of them. If they did die tragically, he may blame himself for antagonizing them and/or for not being there when the accident(s) happened. At any rate, he is bound into a psychological fixation and feels compelled to tell his tale. On the other hand, the fact that he introduces the subject himself suggests that he is working out the complex. The writing of the novel also hints at a capacity for self-healing.

George, the writer and historian, the character who seems least capable of action, turns out to be the potent and controlling force in the play. During the first act and a large part of the second, he endures a series of humiliations, from Martha's attack on his work to her open seduction of a guest. By page 84 he is being physically restrained and his wife is taunting him with the word 'Murderer'. In action, as in passivity, he appears to be a loser. George even jokes with Nick about his supposed failures (pages 28–30). Nevertheless, Martha's leaking of the private fantasy about their son propels George into decisive behaviour. At the end of Act Two he hits on a method of destroying the son myth. What seems to be an act of revenge is really a means of freeing both partners from a cycle of hatred and compensatory sentimentality. Significantly, George incorporates details from his book into the 'death' announcement, as if he were destroying his fantasy as well.

In retrospect one can see that George has been a presiding agent from the beginning of the play: even where he is losing games he is setting up new dramatic encounters. His shotgun and snapdragon devices are ritual preludes to his role as high priest in the latter part of Act Three. The reading of the

Requiem Mass and the parody of Transubstantiation (i.e. change symbolized by bread and wine) underline George's function. He has the power to overturn Martha's fiction because he helped to create that private language and because (as Martha admits) he is the only person who can 'act' in unison with her. A director or master-player has stepped in to shift the action to another level – perhaps a level beyond games. Like his namesake, the first U.S. president, George cannot now tell (or live) a lie. As with Martha, Albee has constructed a character whose contradictions enhance our sense of reality and our pleasure in witnessing it. Moreover, the character is equally interesting on a symbolic or realistic plane: if George stands for an alternative to the usual success myth, he is also – with his dry wit and occasionally explosive gestures – a sharply delineated individual.

Nick

You're ambitious, aren't you, boy?

Nick and Honey serve as opposites to George and Martha. Nick is handsome, athletic and ambitious. He knows exactly what he wants – to rise to the top in academia and gain the necessary status symbols – and he has devised an appropriate strategy for getting there. He has a cool, pragmatic manner which conceals his selfish intentions – until it is stripped away by George. If we feel sorry for Nick when George mocks his overtures of friendship (the abstract painting business, pages 20-21), we gradually come to see the younger man's values for what they are: shallow, ruthless and conformist. During the two conversations between Nick and George (pages 25-32 and 58-74) we get much insight into the former's background and current aims. He has shrewdly calculated the moves which will benefit his career – making the right contacts at one institution, reaping the rewards, then passing on to another. Trapped in a dull relationship, he nevertheless manages to derive advantage from Honey's wealth and normative attitudes. As the play goes on, it becomes evident that Nick is unable to respond to his wife's emotional needs: their existence amounts to a continual evasion of reality.

It has been claimed that Nick's character is 'somewhat underdeveloped'. Responding to this criticism, Albee said that he necessarily had to concentrate on George and Martha, and that a figure like Nick would tread carefully in such a 'power situation' and not be 'terribly loquacious.' This defence seems reasonable. Nick's personality is sufficiently defined for him to be an opposite to George and an active (though secondary) participant in the games ritual. As a biologist he is supposed to typify a mechanical attitude to human behaviour. His habits of objective classification have led him to a disintegrated view of nature. He sees life in black and white, and he only takes risks which are carefully weighed to produce a result. His goals are simple and realizable: material comforts, prestige and power. Unlike George, he does not parade his intellectual views; in fact his subject, biology, is merely a means to other, practical ends. He might just as well be an expert in maths, as Martha and George take him to be, at first. He has no 'Berlin' to defend. Nick cannot understand why George has failed to apply himself to the business of career advancement. Ideas and books seem to him a poor substitute for money and control of an organization. There are many amusing moments where Nick fails to grasp the drift of George's remarks (e.g. pages 25-28 and 67). He is excluded from the private (and shifting) language of the hosts, and he is unable to work out the relation between 'Truth and illusion' (page 119). Only at the end of the play does he begin to perceive what is going on.

It is, of course, necessary that Nick should be attractive in some ways. Martha has picked him out of the crowd of new teachers for post-party entertainment. She is impressed by his youthful, virile manner and by his confident air of achievement (a direct contrast to her husband's image). She is physically drawn to her male guest from the start, and he for his part is excited by the challenge of a flirtation with the college president's daughter. (Martha, we should remember, looks younger than fifty-two, and is 'ample, but not fleshy'.) For a time Nick seems capable of getting his own back on George and of satisfying Martha's desire for manly vigour. However, drink has incapacitated him and, at the beginning of Act Three, he learns what it is like to be on the receiving end of Martha's abuse. She lays into his over-literal attitude to life (page 113) and exposes his coldly opportunist reasons for sexual involvement (page 115). Even taking the consumption of alcohol into account, Nick is not the alert white-hope that he cracks himself up to be. He has made fatal mistakes in the games procedure (e.g. telling George about Honey's hysterical pregnancy) and he has shown himself to be ignorant and insensitive. His occasional hard-hitting shots do not salvage his reputation for health and energy.

Up to George's killing off of the son (page 135), Nick has been naive, unimaginative and calculating. We have felt some sympathy with his plight as a bystander drawn into combat, but on the whole we have looked upon him as a fair target for George's and Martha's assaults. They puncture his pretensions with deadly humour. Nick's attitude to Honey has been protective, condescending and then cruel (see pages 47, 49, 53, and most of Act Two). From page 121 onwards, in Act Three, Nick shows greater concern for his wife. When he discerns Martha's true situation (pages 135-138) he shows a hint of new sensitivity towards Honey. It is possible that the cathartic experience in George's and Martha's house will provide the younger couple with a clearer and more honest basis for relating to one another. Stripped of his cockiness, Nick may be able to guide Honey through a real pregnancy: if he is more involved, perhaps she will not be so frightened of sexual contact.

Honey

Your wife *doesn't* have any hips . . . has she . . . does she?

Honey is the least developed of the four characters because her role demands that she remain a passive spectator for much of the play. However, the main lines of her personality are sketched vividly – through her behaviour and the comments of others. Just as Nick is the antithesis of George, Honey functions as an opposite to Martha. Although she is less intelligent than her husband, Honey forms a logical counterpart to Nick's unquestioning pursuit of materialism. She is the dutiful, dependent female who knows how to advance her husband's career by making the right social contacts. In Kansas, their previous place of residence, she went up to faculty wives in the library and the supermarket and introduced herself. It is she who has persuaded Nick to come to the present get-together (page 20). Honey – the name itself speaks volumes – admires the decor in the house (page 20), compliments Martha on her comedy routine (page 22) and describes the college president as 'a wonderful man' (page 23). She goes on to extol her husband's virtues, where it would be inappropriate for him to do so himself (pages 36–37). She refers proudly to his academic record and his sporting feats.

Honey's well practised manners begin to slip somewhat in the face of George's and Martha's unorthodox entertaining. Although she is not the main butt of the bullying in Act One, Honey shows signs of awkwardness: she cannot name the toilet directly (page 24) and she is shocked by her husband's adoption of strong language (page 47). There is an amusing moment when Honey tries to preserve appearances while Nick is criticizing George on her behalf (page 34). In fact, this 'petite blonde girl' has a dark secret which emerges at the end of Act Two: she is afraid of bearing children and – if George's theory is correct – she takes medicine to stop herself becoming pregnant. The fear of labour is perhaps also a fear of physical involvement with Nick. Threatened by the complications of adult experience, Honey reverts to the role of a child – lying in a foetal position, thumb in her mouth, on the cold bathroom floor (pages 100, 106). Nick explains to George that his 'slim-hipped' wife has a frail constitution which is not conducive to drinking. We see Honey rush out to be sick on two occasions: after George's and Martha's warring duet on page 57, and after George's narration of the 'Blondie' allegory on page 90. She reaches a further stage of panic when George announces the death of the child (pages 134-5). During the 'Walpurgisnacht' of Act Two George unravels her neurosis with uncanny insight.

A hint of Honey's and Nick's child problem – which is paralleled with that of their hosts – emerges on page 34 when George sarcastically asks if they are worried about keeping the babysitter up. Nick reminds him in a kind of warning tone that he and Honey do not have any children. Then in Act Two, when the men are having their intimate but edgy chat, Nick reveals that he married Honey because she was pregnant – or seemed to be, for it turned out to be an illusion. Later he explains that her father was a wealthy preacher and, under George's questioning, he admits that this compensated for the marriage entrapment. The fact that Honey's father was a religious con-man casts an ironic light on her hysterical pregnancy and upright values. Perhaps she is more in control than her 'mousey' appearance (page 14) suggests. At the beginning of the play she seems alert enough to methods of social advancement.

Honey's tendency to throw up becomes a subject of humour in *Virginia Woolf*, but it is a defence mechanism which indicates that she is unwilling to face up to her marriage difficulties or to the things beyond her insular world. Her language is that of a repressed personality – the automatic repetition of the word 'wonderful' (page 23), the long-practised whine (page 33) and the addition of 'Be' to 'ought to' for the sake of correctness (page 43). Like Martha, but with different consequences, Honey has tried to find an identity through her husband's job, and she has been left in a psychological vacuum. Her feeble attempts to be funny are not just a sign of limited intelligence but also a mark of awkward engagement with reality. Nevertheless, at the end of the play Albee holds out a possibility that Honey will undergo a change. The ritual extremes of the night and the contact with Martha's dream (and sterility) have forced her to confront her own fear of childbirth. On page 130 she exclaims that she now wants a child. While this could be an ironic touch, the whole tone of the scene argues for a more positive interpretation. Honey has begun to understand that 'experience' involves an equal measure of pain and joy: that fulfilment cannot be reached without a degree of risk and unpleasantness. As they leave the stage on page 139, she and Nick seem to be on the verge of moving beyond their respective nervousness and detachment. The key to any such change must be emotional honesty.

Themes

The title of the play derives from a graffiti phrase which Albee saw scrawled on the mirror of a New York bar in the 1950s. He took it to mean 'Who's afraid of the big *bad* wolf . . . who's afraid of living life without false illusions.' Virginia Woolf was a famous modern novelist who specialized in describing the inner world of feeling; she fought for the rights of women and, after years of psychological disturbance, committed suicide. Here her name is substituted for the big bad wolf of the nursery rhyme. The title is a riddle which reminds us that people hide behind masks and routines to get through life, but that ultimately reality – with all its unpleasantness – must be faced.

Marriage

On one level the play is a dissection of two marriages, opposite in character but having significant parallels. Both Martha and Honey are childless and have retreated into their private versions of existence. Martha was not able to have any children and she has compensated by inventing a fantasy son. Honey does not want children and has first conjured a fantasy pregnancy and then prevented any real pregnancy occurring. Their respective husbands have – knowingly and unknowingly – sustained these defences against reality: George by entering into the pretence, Nick by failing to look beyond his academic sphere (ironically, biology). Both couples move towards a liberation from their psychological imprisonment. It is an anguished journey and Albee is ruthless in pinpointing the self-delusion and the manipulation which each character resorts to. George and Martha form the main focus of attention, and in their sex-duel Albee exceeds the pyrotechnics of all earlier treatments of the theme, such as Shakespeare's *The Taming of the Shrew* (1593-4) and Strindberg's *The Dance of Death* (1900). As Thomas Porter has pointed out, the situation – a married couple entertaining another couple – resembles that of a Noel Coward drawing-room comedy. But the drama which unfolds is entirely opposite: a savage sequence of laceration down to the marrow. No wonder that audiences have been shocked by this entertainment.

Allegorical significance

Without losing his hold on the particular situation, Albee manages – by various devices – to universalize the experiences portrayed. He has admitted that he named the leading characters George and Martha because 'there is contained within the play ... an attempt to examine the success or failure of American revolutionary principles.' George Washington was the first president of the United States and his wife was called Martha; they were childless; moreover, George, according to the legend, could not tell a lie. Similarly, the university is named New Carthage, which evokes the idea of a great civilization being destroyed.

According to such an allegorical interpretation, the fantasy child would represent the revolutionary principles which have not been realized in American life. Taking a wider sweep, the play could be about the decline of the West. It is significant that George is reading Spengler in Act Two. Albee has even acknowledged a source for Nick in Nikita Krushchev, the former Soviet president, i.e. representative of a totalitarian society. Nevertheless, the playwright has been careful to play down the importance of these larger abstract elements. *Virginia Woolf* is an indictment of American values and attitudes: the success-myth; macho-masculinity; matriarchal tyranny; opportunism; escapism; materialism; relationships based on expediency; and the rejection of sensitivity and inquiry by a philistine group instinct. Yet these concerns grow out of the local human story rather than dictating its structure. Friendship and love, as portrayed here, are the index of a wider civilization or barbarism.

Symbolic effects

The symbols embedded in the play do merit further comment. There are the door-chimes which ring when the guests arrive and when George hurls his book across the room. In a general sense the chimes mark the phases of a ritual. More specifically, they are connected with the removal of the child, since in the Mass bells are rung to indicate that the Host (representing the body of the Son) is about to be lifted up. The extracts from the funeral service tie in with the device of the chimes. For the four characters, and particularly for George and Martha, the last act is a death and a possible resurrection. Albee's introduction of religious elements is subtle; one does not feel that the references are extraneous to the main story. Reading back from the last act, we can see that Martha's description of herself as the Earth Mother carries (ironic) religious overtones: her son is, as it were, virgin-born.

Some critics have found it hard to accept the device of the fantasy child. However, Albee prepares the way for this revelation by the exaggerated behaviour of George and Martha, who carry with them, in extreme form, problems which beset many Americans. The play is at once a satire on, and a sympathetic consideration of, a basic human urge: to live out one's hopes and ideals through one's children. For most couples the raising of children is both an act of generosity and an act of ambition: the selfless giving coexists with the satisfaction of moulding. It is a truism that directing attention outward can take pressure off internal matters (so, the argument goes, having children can save a marriage). George and Martha compensate for their weaknesses by creating an imaginary child. Their differences of outlook and their isolation are covered up – partially – by a shared lie. It seems absurd but it is an adequate stage symbol for a common enough situation: the illusions which we adhere to in order to survive. Albee seems to suggest that we are better off without that falsity: hence the exorcism.

George has his own symbolic instruments which reflect his nature and move the action forward. His trick gun (with the parasol that bursts forth) recalls the story of the boy who shot his mother. By implication this relates to George's sad upbringing. The gun also underlines his rejection of that virile masculinity which Martha says she hungers for. Later in the play George brings another 'weapon' in: the snapdragons. They carry conflicting associations: wedlock, death and fertility. Like a figure from an old romance or fairy story, George comes bearing an agent of change. Out of death may come life.

Social issues

Albee's use of ritual and symbolic elements is given a hard contemporary edge by the presence of social issues. Thus, as a parallel to the failure of communication within marriage there is the division between the life-styles of the two couples. They are temperamentally and functionally opposite. Nick is a scientist and, despite George's over-simplification, he is committed to an attempt to master nature. His opportunism is both personal and professional. George, on the other hand, despises the reduction of life to absolute laws. He refuses to grovel or deceive in order to advance his career. Mechanization and conformity are contrasted with imagination and freedom of the spirit. In a lesser dramatist this theme would be hackneyed, but Albee makes the subject rich by tracing the psychology behind stock attitudes. The two women are also expressive of type. Honey seems, on the surface, to be content with a position of ignorance and subservience; as long as her husband progresses up the ladder, she will be satisfied. Theirs is a marriage based on the bland middle-American dream of material success. Martha, too, yearns for society's badge of approval. Yet her background is not simple enough to allow any such assimilation. She is a frustrated organizer who punishes her husband for the failure to achieve goals that even she can see are three-quarters empty. During the course of the play's games, each marriage and each character has layers of pretence peeled off, like the label on Honey's bottle.

Role-playing and realism

Drawing on a tradition which runs back through Pirandello to Shakespeare and beyond, Albee suggests that reality is akin to the theatrical art itself – in that it changes according to the role and perspective adopted by the participants. George utters the key-statement of the play when he sets up the final game: 'Truth and illusion. Who knows the difference, eh, toots?' (page 119). As spectators, we know more about George than Nick and Honey; yet we don't know for sure whether his stories are literal or symbolic. For this historian, life is not composed of cold objective facts; rather, truth is relative and so-called fictions can be subjective realities. Of course, George is trying to destroy a fundamental illusion – the presence of the child. But he is not against illusion as such. He and his wife make their existence more meaningful by their ability to compose and decompose stories. Albee has it both ways: on the one hand, games and fictions are fanciful, harmful nonsense; on the other, they have a creative place in the interpretation of life. Instead of suppressing the absurdities of acting, the playwright brings his audience face to face with the ways in which 'normality' is simulated. This paradox is at the heart of *Who's Afraid of Virginia Woolf?*

Language and meaning

Language and semantics (investigation into the meaning of words) form a major theme here, as in most of Albee's work. People are shown to judge a situation according to their sense of word associations. George and Martha initiate naming contests in which something more than words is at stake. This is very much in the tradition of riddle-making (as in Norse and Celtic mythology). The games are explicitly linked with language on page 84 when George says, 'We must know other games . . . that can't be the . . . limit of our vocabulary'. Martha calls George 'PHRASEMAKER' (page 16) and he calls her 'a devil with language' (page 20). Linguistic ignorance or misunderstanding are frequent situations in the play. The hosts vie with each other, and with their guests, for word supremacy. For Nick and Honey the problem is that their hosts seems to have a private language which swings from disputation to mutual agreement. The rules of the game seem to be always changing. Nick is the main loser. He cannot follow George's wordplay or abstract terminology, and later he fails to follow Martha's signals. She cannot abide his one-dimensionalism: 'you see all the little specks and crap, but you don't see what goes on' (page 113). Among the various instances of word combat, word confusion and word magic are: the name of the Bette Davis film (pages 11-13); Maths/Biology (pages 28-29); 'floozie' (page 50); 'sick' (page 60); 'gaggle' (page 71); 'novel' (page 83); 'snap' (pages 95, 119–120); 'microphone' (page 113). When Nick tells George that he and Honey will 'stay' in New Carthage, the older man qualifies this with 'every definition has its limits' (page 31). His remark might well stand for the whole process of communication in the play.

Conclusion

It is evident then that the themes of *Virginia Woolf* are rooted in its linguistic structure. As in all great literature, form and content are intertwined. Albee's drama is a witty and profound commentary on life in the western world during the second half of the twentieth century. Even though the playwright has expressed admiration for recent developments in university education (such as the study of contemporary drama), his portrait of New Carthage remains an indictment of our civilization. At the same time one must stress the life-affirming nature of the play's conclusion; Albee's vision is not entirely negative. Unlike

the figures in pure absurd drama, George and Martha experience change – a purgation of ills and the promise of a more
meaningful existence. Marriage is not necessarily a prison of
emotional sterility; it can be the cutting edge where honesty
begins.

Structure

The structure of *Virginia Woolf*, as well as its atmosphere, is tragi-comic: that is to say, it moves through disorder and loss to a (partial) discovery of identity. The play's intimation of rebirth, and its raw humour up to that point, prevent it being a tragedy; likewise, the qualified character of the conclusion, and the extent of disruption portrayed in the play, prevent it being wholly a comedy. Following Northrop Frye's division of forms in *Anatomy of Criticism*, one might describe the work as an ironic comedy.

Ritual

The origins of drama are thought to lie in vegetation ritual, whereby a part of life is cut off to bring greater unity and health to the main body of nature. Ancient ceremonies in the Mediterranean world involved the worship of a being who represented the principle of growth, decay and rebirth. Mythologists have called him the Year-Daemon or Vegetation Spirit. Such a ritual had regular phases: 1) an *agon*, or sacred combat, between the old god (or king or hero) and the new; 2) a *sparagmos*, in which the victim was literally or symbolically torn asunder; 3) the delivery of this news by a messenger; 4) lamentation and/or rejoicing by the onlookers. Further stages might be: the finding of the hidden or dismembered spirit; and his epiphany or resurrection. Dionysos, Osiris, Attis and Adonis are all forms of the dying god; even Christ may be said to conform to this pattern. The Festival of Dionysos included rites of passage, celebrating stages in the growth of the individual and of society. Pain and happiness were intertwined.

In the twentieth century there have been attempts to reintroduce this ritual into drama, T. S. Eliot's *The Cocktail Party* being a notable example. Working from a less intellectual position and with different models, Antonin Artaud (1896–1948) has also brought back mysteries and rites to the stage. This French actor, director and playwright argued that the theatre needed to recover the cruel, disturbing elements which had gripped and transformed the consciousness of participants in ancient ceremonies. Such dark powers, he said, could summon up 'a bloodstream of images' to dispel pretence and purify the spectator's sensibility. Significantly, he spoke of 'an exorcism to make our demons FLOW.' The first translation of Artaud's *The Theatre and its Double* was published in New York in 1958. There can be little doubt that Albee read this and linked the ideas with his experience of drama.

Theatrical currents

Who's Afraid of Virginia Woolf? is, in fact, a meeting point for many theatrical currents: religious ritual; the theatre of cruelty; absurdist alienation; expressionism; social satire; and the naturalistic drawing-room comedy. Dealing for the moment with ritual, we should observe that the structure of Albee's play is similar to that involving the Year-Daemon. There is a party at which the older teacher battles with the younger one; George becomes a victim but recovers his supremacy in the last act; the true victim turns out to be the fantasy child, news of whose death is delivered by a messenger (according to George's description); the fantasy is torn apart; there is lamentation but also a feeling of relief and hope among the participants. The four characters and particularly Martha have undergone a rite of passage, leading to a new self-awareness.

Verbal allusions

Not only in the plot but also in verbal allusions, Albee attempts to give his play a ritualistic thrust: for example, the description of the son as a 'bean bag' recalls the scattering of the Corn God seed (i.e. body) over the earth. On the other hand, the playwright is not slavish in his adherence to this pattern. One can discern other mythic elements in the drama: Martha, for instance, seems to be a displaced earth-mother – the figure who brings regeneration by coupling with the young god or spirit. Alan Schneider, the director of the first production, has described *Virginia Woolf* as a 'phantasmagoria' – a term reminiscent of Artaud's attempt to bring into being 'a real dream ... on stage.' The atmosphere of exaggerated antagonism in Albee's play is close to that sought by the French writer. Moreover, each act is assigned a title which indicates that a primitive rite is taking place: 'Fun and Games' (preliminary sport and sparring); 'Walpurgisnacht' (the gathering of the menacing spirits); 'The Exorcism' (the expulsion of the spirits). The last title was originally applied to the play as a whole, which shows which way Albee's mind was tending. One can see that the sequence is cumulative, so that each phase is more intense.

Games

What makes *Virginia Woolf* strikingly effective as ritual is the author's use of games as a basis for action. In one step Albee solves the problem of how to make ritual relevant to the modern age: the games are at once artificial devices and real psychological manaoeuvres. Albee formalizes the process by which adults entertain and compete with one another – a system which can be observed in purer form among children. Iona and Peter Opie, in *Children's Games in Street and Playground* (1969), divide games into the following categories: chasing; catching; seeking; hunting; racing; duelling; exerting; daring; guessing; acting; and pretending. Clearly in the adult world sexual motivation is more likely to come to the fore, and levels of pretence are more sophisticated. Nevertheless, the games which adults play do reflect the codes and devices of childhood.

Four main games are played in *Virginia Woolf*; 'Humiliate the host'; 'Get the Guests'; 'Hump the Hostess'; and 'Bringing Up Baby'. These are all power conflicts and they double as entertainment and punishment. At various points each character inflicts pain on another or others, and is in turn the object of bullying (usually verbal). Each game has its own rules, which are liable to change without notice. During each phase somebody's inner world or past experience is investigated. Thus in the first game George's stagnation in the academic world is emphasized; then his aspiration to be a novelist is ridiculed; finally, his imaginative concerns are exposed when Martha suggests that his novel was autobiographical. In the second game George retaliates by narrating a fable which brings out the darker secrets of Nick's and Honey's marriage. In the third game Martha tries to emasculate and dispossess George by having sexual intercourse with Nick – in the course of which the latter's limitations are revealed. George affects unconcern but is rattled. In the fourth game Martha's inner secret is unravelled and her fantasy destroyed. The first victim is now the victor, although his act of destruction has a healing aspect.

Such a summary does not do justice to the subtle way in which Albee allows each character to attain degrees of ascendancy and inferiority within a particular phase. George has moments of power in the first Game, while Martha preserves a certain dignity in the last one. Again, there are rest periods when the game procedures cease to operate. Gilbert Debusscher has observed that as the play develops the games span becomes longer and more intense, while the periods of 'reality' get shorter. Albee goes through the full range of game structures from satirical and nonsense rhymes to information or naming contests and, ultimately, physical combat. There are riddles, truth tests and all manner of tricks and traps. Among the strategies adopted are: correctives, insults and ambiguous answers; parody and impropriety; bargain making; conspiracy; ostentation; flattery and flirtation; deceit; intimidation; scission; diversion; evasion; pacification; retreat and open attack. Since American culture places great value on success in games and sport, Albee's play becomes an ironic commentary upon the means by which people gain approval in society. Behind the façade of absolute rules in a game, there is no standard against which behaviour can be judged.

The games situation allows Albee to weave extremities into an ordinary setting. Alan Schneider has spoken of how, in the original production, a balance was struck between realistic decor (period furniture, bookshelves, hi-fi system) and symbolic elements. The set had strange angles and planes built in to cause distortion. Albee wanted the living-room to have a womb or cave aspect. In other productions this abstraction has been emphasized further, but Albee has stated that he prefers a quasi-naturalistic arrangement. The universal meaning was, in fact, suggested by certain details in the Broadway set, such as an American flag and a colonial eagle. Modern comforts were framed by the insignia of past ideals.

Literal and allegorical

Some critics have claimed that the allegorical or symbolic elements are not fully worked out in *Virginia Woolf*. They have objected to the way in which the story of the asylum boy (= the country's twisted childhood) is undercut by the direct identification with George; to Martha's open seduction of Nick; to the device of the fantasy child; and to the portrayal of college life — on the grounds that these are all incredible. However, the history of the play's performance seems to justify Albee's method. Audiences have been mystified and intrigued but not betrayed. The realism of the play's language and characterization does not necessarily demand a literal interpretation of events. Again, complete synthesis may not be desirable here: the absurdist in Albee wishes to keep meanings open-ended (a sure enough dramatic instinct).

Analogy with music

Evidence of careful deployment of materials is to be found in Albee's often repeated statement that play construction and musical composition are similar. Alan Schneider has observed that *Virginia Woolf* is organized almost as a symphonic score 'with rhythmical repetitions of elements' and themes which come in and out with varying intensity. At the time of the production, he says, Albee was very concerned with the rhythm and tempo of each scene. Indeed, the more one examines the play the more formally patterned it becomes. To start with there are the opposite ideologies of the men, the pregnancy/birth fantasies of the women, and even the syllabic equivalence of the names (male one syllable; female two). Nick and Honey are, in some ways, mere witnesses of the sado-masochistic game between George and Martha; yet their position and their comments drive the action forward. Albee has called the younger couple 'a motivating audience'. Each character plays a part in the exposition, development and recapitulation of themes. George has a dialogue with Nick in which things are found out that – made public – reduce Honey to physical sickness. Later George enlists Honey's help in killing off the fantasy child, which brings Martha to a state of despair. Talking to Honey off-stage, Martha reveals the existence of the son, which leads George to feel betrayed. Martha's adultery with Nick induces George to 'murder' the child. The second and fourth examples mentioned take place simultaneously: while Nick and Martha simulate procreation off-stage, George and Honey are arranging a death sequence on stage. Another example of dovetailing is the emergence and re-emergence of George's story about the car accident (see pages 62, 83, 135).

Unity

The pacing of each act is different but there is an underlying unity of purpose. Act One contains mostly ensemble-grouping, with some one-to-one and threesome interludes. The lid is taken off the convention of party small-talk and one character, George, is humiliated. Exchanges which have a quick-fire lightness begin to carry a tragic undertone. Act Two, the longest, is more varied in terms of grouping: there is a long dialogue between Nick and George, a phase in which Martha and Nick get closer (they are alone for a short spell); and a dialogue between George and Honey. The contest between Nick and George seems a spin-off from the rivalry between George and Martha. The action reaches an extreme in George's attempt to throttle Martha and in her seduction of Nick while George is present. Act Three is the shortest but it proceeds at a slower pace. Martha has two long speeches, one a monologue. George controls the pace, building up a dual narrative with ritualistic shape. After the houseboy business, Nick and Honey seem almost peripheral. The 'death' scene is zany enough on one level – the overlay of extracts from the mass on Martha's account of her son's upbringing. But irony has replaced satire as the central mode.

Tableau-building

In the section on 'Themes' it was noted that Albee is much concerned with the play elements in life. In *Virginia Woolf* George and Martha present their fiction almost as a stage show, changing the scene – the version of reality – as they go along. This tableau-building becomes a dominant feature in the second half of Act Three. It is an old device (Shakespeare was fond of it), yet it makes absolute sense here as a summation of twentieth-century illusion. The dismantling of the 'show' is an appropriate means of returning the theatre audience to reality. Albee proves that he knows about the nuts and bolts of playmaking, as well as its inner spirit.

Conclusion

Virginia Woolf is composed mainly of words rather than actions (although it might be said that the words have a sculptural, bodied quality). Pieces of physical behaviour are thereby thrown into greater prominence, and there are moments when the ritual implicit in Albee's pattern comes sharply into focus. George, the dispenser of alcohol (an agent of transformation), is the main instigator of effects: he 'shoots' a gun, breaks a bottle, puts on records, tries to strangle his wife, hurls a book at the chimes, appears with snapdragons which he uses as spears. This can be seen as reactive behaviour but George's shock-moves are surely an ironic reflection on his supposed impotence as a man of thought. Martha, too, has her share of vital actions: she changes her clothes, dances intimately with Nick and twines him about her on a chair. Nick plays his part in this and Honey has her vomiting fits, but the guests are essentially passive in relation to their hosts.

Throughout the play the singing of the 'Virginia Woolf' song serves as a binding motif (it appears at pages 15, 22, 57, 99 and 140). It embodies the terror and humour which Albee so successfully fuses in this ritual entertainment.

Style

Introduction

Albee's plays tend to rely more on talking than action. Thus an examination of his linguistic procedures in *Virginia Woolf* is particularly necessary for an understanding of the play. One's first reaction is likely to be that the language is raw and the rhythms hard. Certainly, there is a good deal of gutsy abuse from the opening expletive onwards. Martha and George are habituated to such a mode of address (it is part of their games technique); Nick's and Honey's language is plainer and more polite, although they are gradually drawn into the area of verbal fireworks. By page 48 even Honey is saying, 'When's the little bugger coming home?' George, on this first night of their meeting, calls her 'angel-tits' and 'monkey-nipples' (page 80). The vitriolic exchanges of the older couple have great dramatic intensity (e.g. pages 94–95) and no doubt had more shock value in 1962. Albee creates a kind of poetry out of vulgar and commonplace phrases (e.g. 'sprung a leak'); and he reintroduces to cliché some of the freshness of original metaphor.

Qualities of dialogue

It has been observed by Harold Clurman that Albee's realistic-sounding dialogue is actually 'a highly literate and full-bodied distillation of common American speech.' In other words, the colloquial idiom has been heightened to make it a more precise instrument. Nobody speaks quite like this in real life, but for a realistic impression to be created in the theatre some modification is required. Albee creates a delicate balance between outright absurdity and credible behaviour. Much of what sounds spontaneous is organized rhetorically. George, of course, is the kind of person who, in telling a tale or making a point, will artfully use the most expressive means of delivery. His upbringing and his job have ensured that such tricks of speech are second nature to him. He does a special line in refined vulgarity (honed by years of practice with Martha, one assumes). Much of his talk is measured and witty: the description of Martha's father (pages 31–32); the description of Nick's ambitions (page 45); and the pointed allegory recounted in Act Two (pages 86-9). Martha says that she finds his intellectual manner 'convoluted' (page 93) but at other times she shows appreciation of her husband's verbal dexterity. George's humour can seem slightly displaced (e.g. page 99), as if he is speaking on another level from that of his listeners, but this is often a calculated effect. More will be said about that when we consider irony.

Martha's manner of speech is direct and down to earth; in fact it is complementary to George's style. From a dramatic point of view they are effective foils for one another. In Acts One and Two, Martha's conversation pulses with ferocious energy; she is the driving force behind the action. From the stabbing insistence of her opening remarks to George, to the easy rhythms of her account of husband-hunting (page 53), and the tired description of rupture (pages 94-95), she provokes the other characters into more animated performance. This is despite George's function as drink-dispenser and grand commentator. Martha's language changes in Act Three: she gains a new lyricism and warmth (particularly evident in her speech at the top of page 113), Albee takes a risk here in opening out her character through a new style of speech. However, the use of rhetoric is justified in terms of the playwright's larger ends and it works well in the theatre.

As already indicated, Nick and Honey speak in a less extravagant fashion than their hosts. Nevertheless, there moments when they are assigned a richer style (e.g. Nick's comments on pages 68-69 and Honey's on pages 104-105). Each of them has an individualized tone which Albee can sustain, intensify or depart from at key points in the play. Nick's predominant register is cool and matter-of-fact, with an edge of subdued vigour. Honey's manner is hesitant and insipid, with streaks of clichéd sentimentality. Albee deftly catches the slips and slurs which alcohol can induce in ordinary speech.

Diction and rhythm

Who's Afraid of Virginia Woolf? contains a wide range of diction and rhythm, considering that there are only four characters. The language swings from the poetic to the banal, from lyricism to crudeness and profanity, from the effusive to the monosyllabic. What makes the text memorable and effective is the way in which these styles interact with one another. Albee's sense of timing is astute, as where Honey re-enters after the book-throwing incident in Act Two. As befits a games situation, words are uttered as part of a continual layering process: even George's and Martha's non-sequiturs seem to find an echo or resolution in later statements. The language of the play is energized by explosions and dissonance, yet there are also instances of harmony, bitter-edged but indicative of a calmer way of living. The duet device has already been commented upon; it occurs at moments of conflict, and is therefore ironic, but it does have a unifying potential.

Comedy

Albee has, on various occasions, stressed the comic dimension of the play. After he directed a revival in 1976 he said: 'I tried to emphasize the fact that George and Martha enjoyed their verbal duels with each other, and while they were deadly serious, they were always at the same time in admiration of each other's skills'. He spoke of the 'sense of glee' that the two characters have in what they are doing. Some readers and spectators might be surprised by these remarks. However, the play can be humorous in perform-ance: the situations and dialogue are at once painful and enter-taining. George's speeches contain witty wordplay, and Martha, who claims she doesn't have a sense of humour (page 51), draws laughter by her fiery exhibitionism. The two guests excite mirth through their failure to understand or match the games language of their hosts. A good example of theatrical humour is George's request that Nick dump the snapdragons 'in some gin' (page 117). This comic element makes the cruelty and savagery bearable, and it prepares the way for a possible reconciliation.

Irony

A main stylistic vehicle in the play is irony. George is particularly adept at conveying disapproval by oblique means, for example when he homes in on Nick's smug values. Martha's more charac-teristic weapon is satire, for example when she taunts George about his low salary (page 56). For a play which seems so raw in style, there is a remarkable amount of learned allusion in the text. George's comments to Nick on page 31, for instance, depend upon a knowledge of Shakespeare, Anatole France, the Bible and classi-cal history. There is throughout *Virginia Woolf* an appeal to the audience's sense of intellectual superiority: much of the games activity could be described as a battle for knowledge, and our 'pleasure' in witnessing these contests derives partly from a pri-vileged position of understanding.

Imagery

Albee's play is rich in imagery – even down to the stage directions ('defending herself against an attack of bees', page 134). The careful structuring of scenic and verbal images again recalls musical composition. The cycle of excitement and sorrow which characterizes George's and Martha's relationship is vividly encapsulated by the latter in the image of the ice cubes which have been solidified only to melt again – a reflection which comes to her as she jiggles the ice in her glass (page 110). This harks back to the conversation about ice cubes on page 16, as well as George's remarks on page 99. The removal of illusion is signalled first by Martha's snapping of her fingers and play on the word 'snap' (pages 94-95). This image is picked up by George when he brings in a bunch of snapdragons and throws them at Martha and Nick (pages 115–121). He snaps his fingers too and, in uttering the word 'snap', echoes Martha's habitually snappish manner.

The image of the son has been discussed under the section on Themes. It will suffice to say here that the device is a bold one which is neatly introduced and unfolded. Like the title image 'Virginia Woolf', it retains a residue of mystery. Other significant images are: the door chimes; the huckleberry bush; the bottle labels; the parasol-shotgun; the car accident and the porcupine; chromosomes; and the day of judgement. Each game engenders a cluster of lesser images, as well as ringing changes on the main ones.

Conclusion

To sum up, the language employed by Albee in *Virginia Woolf* is arranged so as to produce the impression of spontaneity. George and Martha, especially, seem able to take off into new regions at the slightest stimulus. The dialogue is colloquial but this freedom is underpinned by rhetoric. A tension is sustained between glossy and rough elements of speech (a necessary accompaniment to the ritual plot structure). According to the emotional requirements of a scene, the language can be sharp and lean or rounded and full. If much of the play seems to be about failed or imprisoned communication, the words used to express that breakdown and distortion are evocative – conveying a clear picture of extreme experience.

General questions

1 Consider the presence and effect of allegorical and symbolic elements in *Virginia Woolf*. Is the play anything more than a story of four individuals whose marital relations are shaky?

Guideline notes

Introduction – setting, New Carthage – characters representing types in American history and society – framework indicated by act titles.

The fantasy child – significance – social, religious and psychological implications – way introduced and developed.

Elements woven into the games – George's two allegories – the bergin boy, Blondie and his frau – Martha's response – links – fable-like way of describing experience, sometimes ironic – use of devices such as trick gun and snapdragons. Other symbols – the chimes, the brandy bottle. Connexions with ritual. Learned allusions.

Realism of behaviour – despite stylized portrayal and exaggeration. Details which ring true – physical and verbal responses – fleshed out characters – exact stage directions.

Conclusion – balance struck between the particular and the universal, between the modern and the ancient/eternal. Profound issues of life – the history/biology debate – the function of children – nature of marriage – mental development – relevance of the play to our time – how to stage the symbolic successfully – refer to the film – significance of the title – a deep theme based on a common rhyme.

2 Do you think that Albee's play contains any philosophical or social message?

3 What are the main themes of *Virginia Woolf*?

4 Explain the significance of the play's title.

5 'Obsessed with the negative aspects of human behaviour.' How far would you agree with this judgement of *Virginia Woolf*?

6 Give a detailed account of the way in which the relationship between George and Martha is presented.

7 Do you feel that the characters of the two guests are sufficiently developed?

8 Explore the parallels and contrasts between the two couples in the play.

9 'A sophisticated analysis wrapped up as popular entertainment.' Comment on this view of *Who's Afraid of Virginia Woolf?*

10 Analyse the structure of the play, paying particular attention to the pacing of each act.

11 To what extent is *Who's Afraid of Virginia Woolf?* a comedy?

12 What is the function of games in *Virginia Woolf?*

13 How successful is the device of the imaginary son?

14 Discuss Albee's use of irony and satire in *Virginia Woolf*.

15 What qualities of language make *Virginia Woolf* effective as a drama?

Further reading

Richard Amacher: *Edward Albee* (rev. edn., Twayne Publishers 1982)

C. W. E. Bigsby: *Albee* (Oliver & Boyd 1969)

Ruby Cohn: *Edward Albee* (University of Minnesota Press 1969)

Gilbert Debusscher: *Edward Albee: Tradition and Renewal* (Center for American Studies, Brussells 1969)

Ronald Hayman: *Edward Albee* (Heinemann Educational Books 1971)

Margaret Murray: *The God of the Witches* (Sampson, Low, Marston 1930)

Anna Paolucci: *Edward Albee* (Southern Illinois University Press 1972)

Thomas E. Porter: *Myth and Modern American Drama* (Wayne State University Press 1969)

Alan Schneider: essays in C. W. E. Bigsby: *A Collection of Critical Essays (Prentice-Hall 1975)*

Anita Maria Stenz: Edward Albee: the Poet of Loss (Mouton Publishers 1978)